Esquire Publications
13720 Old Saint Augustine Road #8-322
Jacksonville, FL 32258-7414
www.esquirepublications.com
Tel: 1-800-501-7640

"The Adventures of an Italian American Chef: A Memoir with Recipes"

Edited By: Georgia Editing Service, LLC.

Book and Cover Design By
Designs Unparallel, LLC
www.designsunparallel.net

Library of Congress Control Number: 2023912854
ISBN: 978-1-7376918-9-1

Prelude

I had the opportunity many years ago to do a cookbook. In fact, with the assistance of a gentleman (the vice president of Tiffany's in Kansas City), I could have used some of the China and Silverware from Napoleon's traveling collection. Being young and dumb, I said no thanks. Some 30-plus years later, I had a second chance to do a cooking-type book. I had a few requirements. First, I am retired, and wanted to write a fun book. Yes, there are recipes of all kinds from my various adventures, but my travels cover almost all of the USA, and the Caribbean.

Instead of a cookbook, I have written a biographical story of my life with many recipes from each stop along the way.

Enjoy!

Acknowledgments

It is easy to say someone's career would not have been as successful if it weren't for a specific mentor. In my case, I was fortunate to have someone in my corner relatively early in my career in 1987. I was interviewed and hired by Michael Gibson. At the time, Michael was the general manager of the Holiday Inn World's Fair site in downtown Knoxville, TN. This was a high-volume corporate hotel in direct competition with a Hilton Hotel, a Hyatt, and an on/off again Ramada Renaissance. This hotel was built in 1982, specifically for the World's Fair. It was also located just one block from the University of Tennessee in Knoxville. As a result, the professional image our hotel staff had to put forward was pressure-filled.

During my tenure, Michael patiently taught me by instruction, as well as by example through his words and deeds on how to run a successful department (it was Food and Beverage Department). Michael showed me the importance of building a team that worked as one unit. To accomplish these tasks, our team members had to feel their input/ideas were listened to, and in some cases implemented. The team also needed to feel there were future possibilities for advancement. Michael once told me the largest dissatisfiers among young managers in the hospitality industry work the long hours, that it was our responsibility to show managers/supervisors how to organize themselves in their thoughts and actions to reduce the length of their days. Little tasks like writing your daily tasks on 3" x 5" index cards. At the end of the day, check off all that was accomplished, then do a new card for the next shift. We would add the items not completed, plus the next day's tasks. This practice increased efficiency, reduced hours to conduct little daily five -minute meetings with your sub departments communications – was the "most important" aspect of management. Talking about communication is one thing, but managers that follow through with comprehensive daily communication is rare, the largest associate complaints these days is through with comprehensive daily communication is rare, the largest associate complaints these days is that no one communications plans to them on.

Lastly, I am so grateful I was shown to prepare a budget, create a proforma, learn management skills, which are not taught today. Instead, corporate does the budgets, in some cases, prepares schedules in short, through the failure of our education system, corporations have made operational management more of a "no brainer."

So, Michael, thank you for your introduction to management 101 (AKA Common Sense Management)

CHAPTER 1

The Early Years

When I was 7-years old, I was a member of the cub scouts. I enjoyed camping out but was not a fan of hiking (exercise was not my vision of fun). To get the badges that I needed, I would perform tasks like cooking breakfast for my parents. It just became easy to flip eggs in the pan without breaking them in the process. "Hey, this is fun!" I realized. I would then make dishes that required following a recipe. When I was 8-years old, our teacher asked the class to bring in recipes to make a "Mother's Day Cookbook." Of course, everyone in class brought in a cookie, cake, or candy recipe, except for me. I brought in a recipe for Hot German Potato Salad. My mother kept the book in her safekeeping. Photos, report cards, etc. I began using all the spices in the cupboard. At one point, I began critiquing my mother's cooking ability, at which point she suggested I keep my opinions to myself. I hadn't learned the art of diplomacy yet.

In my 12th year of life, I entered the baking competition at the fair. I baked a chocolate oil cake, and of course, my favorite chocolate chip cookies. I took away two blue ribbons. It's amazing some of the looks and comments I received from the ladies in the bake off (some were not flattering or kind). I did acquire a lot of new friends in my class, however. The cake and cookies were inhaled within minutes of the baking results.

At age 17, our church had their annual BBQ. It was a large event; some 1,400 people would attend and support this event. Of course, I had no experience pulling off an event this size, but I was brash and cocky.

The first night, we got together to discuss how to pull off this undertaking. The men all came with the potato peelers their wives had loaned them. Again, being brash, I spoke up and said I wasn't going to peel 400 lb. of potatoes for the potato salad. There had to be an easier way. A couple days before the BBQ, the soldiers from Fort Devens, Ayer, M.A., were setting up the grills, tables, etc. I asked the sergeant in charge if I could use the army mess kitchen to peel and cook the 8 cases of potatoes. In less than three hours, this task was completed! The other men at church were impressed so they listened to my ideas about the rest of the menu. I ordered 1400 half chickens, made the BBQ sauce, potato salad dressing and the salad dressing from scratch.

At that point, the men were asking my advice, some old enough to be my grandfather. On the Sunday of the event, the entire 1400 chickens were grilled and ready for consumption before the first person came through the buffet line. The next Sunday, our pastor told the congregation that they had the most successful BBQ ever and not a single piece of chicken came back due to not being fully cooked. He also stated that he received many compliments on the affair. The next year was even bigger!

Going back a bit, my family moved from upstate New York when I was 13-years old. My father was a civilian working for the US Air Force. In 1964, he was transferred to Hanscom AFB in Bedford, MA. This was not a good time in my scholastic career. The high school I went to in Littleton, MA was not as progressive as the school I attended in upstate New York. I began to rebel against the establishment. Administration put me in remedial classes. I tried to tell my teachers and guidance counselors that I took algebra and geometry in New York, but I was placed in a math class where they were still studying addition and subtraction. I got nowhere. To emphasis this issue, I sat on the bench in the office during my scheduled math class. The principal called my parents and scheduled a meeting. The meeting was slightly successful. I was moved up one peg to the higher remedial class where they were studying multiplication and division. After that, I lost interest in school. I was disgusted with the administration. As a junior, I organized a food strike in the cafeteria. I was beginning to learn how to organize people and improve my negotiating skills. We won our fight, and the cafeteria manager agreed to improve the menus and selections. The next year, I became the chairperson of the prom committee and yearbook committee. Both turned out very successful, but it took a lot of work.

Upon graduation, I was accepted into community college with one stipulation, I had to attend summer school. My grades were so poor, the college wanted me to prove I was worthy of college. For the first time since junior high, I was scholastically motivated. I aced all my courses and was accepted as a freshman. The one great thing I picked up from summer school was to focus on my goals. Several of my summer school classmates and I ran for student government. We all won our contests, and I gave my first speech when I ran with newly found speech skills. I was elected treasurer of the student government. With the math skills I had developed on my own, I was able to allocate student activities, money to cover all the clubs and organizations and have money left over for a big party at the end of the school year. During my tenure on the student government, I also was the news editor of the college newspaper, as well as becoming the head of student security. We took some of the extra money and purchased a patrol car for the security guards.

Being astute with the financial aspect of student government, I noticed the president of the college received a percentage of the money from the student activity fees. It was supposed to be used to entertain the dignitaries for dinner and for public relations. We found out that the president was instead taking his family and friends out to dinner and bought his family Christmas tree with those funds. With the assistance of a couple other editors of the newspaper and the officials of the student government, we traveled to the state capital, Boston, and gave the state attorney general this information. Again, the results were positive. The president was placed on probation, and the "Slush Fund" was returned to the student treasury. From that point forward, my colleagues and I were referred to as "members of the Lunatic Fringe," and "Pot Smoking, Beer Drinking Hippies!"

My college career spanned six years to acquire two associated degrees (2-year degrees). The first degree in business, the second in culinary arts. I was fortunate to attend culinary school in Boston. I was training to be a cook at a club called Pleasant Valley Community Club. I did prep work, line cooking, and short order cooking. In the evening, I attended my classes. I had the benefit of learning old school, as well as "new school" cooking. The head instructor had also been the captain of the American Team in the Cooking Olympics held every four years, similar to the Olympics. I learned quickly, the chef at the Country Club and the Head Instructor were close friends. There was no BS with either man, and I was tested by both on the curriculums. Oh, did I say Pleasant Valley Country Club was the only stop in New England for the PGA at that time?

THE ORIGINAL
Riverfront
BARBECUE OPEN

WINNERS

GRAND CHAMPION - Art Rodenberg, "Cooking Cousins", Ballwin MO

1st PLACE CHICKEN - Dick Spoon, Cheshire Inn, St. Louis, 63117

1st PLACE BEEF - Richard Vanderburg, "Hog Heaven Cookers" O'Fallon IL, 62269

1st PLACE PORK - Billy Bolyard, "Uncle Billy's BBQ Baste" St. Charles, 63301

SHOWMANSHIP - Rick Stofferahn "Rick's Chicks" St. Louis, 63144

FINALISTS

CHICKEN

Dick Spoon, Chesire Inn, 63117
Keith Bosso, "Willie's", Fenton
Neil Thompson, House of Jamica, 63130
Bahrami Bershid, Little Kitchen, 63101
Richard Vanderburg, "Hog Heaven Cookers", O'Fallon IL
Joyce Hofer, Hofer's, Dupo, IL 62239
Carl Huck, Muddy Waters, 63102

BEEF

Richard Vanderburg, "Hog Heaven Cookers", O'Fallon, IL
Steve Wehele, Gosen's Tavern, Rhineland, 65069
Diane Strader, Roy & Diane Strader, Edwardsville, IL
Terry McKean, Andria's, O'Fallon, IL

PORK

Billy Bolyard, "Uncle Billy's BBQ Baste", St. Charles
Art Rodenburg, "Cooking Cousins" Ballwin, 63021
Mike Emerson, St. Louis Area Nephrology Tech's (S.L.A.N.T.)
Mark Savage, "Construction Que", Farmington, 63640

 Presented as a benefit for
NATIONAL KIDNEY FOUNDATION of Eastern Missouri and Metro East, Inc.
225 South Meramec Avenue, Suite 200
St. Louis, Missouri 63105

(314) 863-5858

Escarole Soup
(makes 1 gallon)

Ingredients:

1 lb. hot Italian sausage, cut into ½" rounds

½ lb. boneless chicken thighs, cut into ½" pieces

1 bunch escarole chopped

1 cup navy beans soaked

½ cup ditalini pasta

2 med carrots diced into ¼" pieces

2 stalks celery cut into ¼" pieces

2 qt. chicken stock

½ cup grated Parmesan cheese

3 tbsp. Lea & Perrins Worcestershire sauce

Cracked black pepper to taste

2 tsp. dried basil

3 tbsp. olive oil

Method:

Soak the beans overnight in a soup pot. The next day, cook the beans until they are tender. In a frying pan, heat the olive oil, and place the cut sausage until it browns. Add to the beans. In the same frying pan, brown the chicken, add to the soup pot. Lastly, sauté the celery, carrots, and onions in drippings of meat. Add to the same pot, including drippings. Simmer for 30 minutes then add all the seasonings and pasta. The beans and pasta will thicken up the soup. Add the stock and lastly, the escarole and cheese. Simmer for 15 minutes. Serve with hot garlic bread to soak up the soup and enjoy!

A traditional first course in an Italian Sunday family dinner

Mama's Tomato Mozzarella Salad
(Serves 2 – 4)

Ingredients:

2 sliced yellow tomatoes

2 sliced red tomatoes

4 sliced buffalo mozzarella

½ cup shredded lettuce

Fresh basil, chopped

Balsamic vinegar

Extra virgin olive oil

Salt and pepper to taste

Method:

On top of shredded lettuce, stack, and rotate tomato, then cheese and repeat until all are stacked around the plate. Then sprinkle with fresh basil and drizzle with Balsamic Vinegar, olive oil, salt, and pepper.

A light summer salad goes well with grilled food or roasts cooked in the oven.

Aunt Ida's Chicken Salad Boat
(Serves 4)

Ingredients:

5 oz. chicken salad mixture (see recipe)

Dug out pineapple (with leaves) (¼ Each)

4 oz. Each additional sliced fruit

4 leaves green or red kale

1 tsp. chopped parsley

Method:
On a dinner plate, place ale (garnish), then place quartered pineapple on top. Add chicken salad inside pineapple. Slice all fruit and arrange on plate, then sprinkle parsley overall.

Sage Dressing
(makes approximately 15 servings)

Ingredients:

2 loaves of stale bread

1 large Spanish onion (diced)

1 celery heart (diced)

2 qt. chicken stock

1 tbsp. rubbed sage

¼ cup Lea & Perrins

4 eggs

Salt and pepper to taste

1 tbsp. poultry seasoning

3 tbsp. margarine

Method:

Tear up bread by hand into large mixing bowl. In a salute pan, melt butter, and sauté onions and celery until tender. Then place into mixing bowl. Crack eggs and add rest of spices and chicken stock. Mix thoroughly. Dressing should be moist, not watery. Place into baking pan and bake at 350° F for 30 – 45 minutes until firm and brown on top.

This dressing goes well with the stuffed pork chops with sautéed apples or your turkey at Thanksgiving

Warm German Potato Salad
(Serves 8)

Ingredients:

4 large Idaho potatoes (do not peel)

12 oz. bacon, diced up coarsely

2 stalks celery finely chopped

¼ red onion finely chopped

½ bunch green onions coarsely chopped

Salt and pepper to taste

2 oz. dill pickle juice

1 medium dill pickle

1/8 cup extra virgin olive oil

¼ cup cider vinegar

2 tbsp. Lea & Perrins

½ tsp. granulated garlic

1 tsp. dill weed

2 qt. water

Method:

In a large sauce pot, bring water to boil and add 1 tbsp. salt. Cook potatoes until fork tender. Rinse off with cold water in colander. Drain and put into large salad bowl. In a skillet, brown off bacon, then take out of bacon drippings to drain. Reserve bacon drippings in sauté pan. Add all seasonings and mix thoroughly with burner turned off. Add celery, onion, bacon, and green onion to potatoes, then add all ingredients in skillet. Mix thoroughly. Serve warm.

It's so different from mayor mustard-based potato salads. Bacon makes everything better!

Grandma's Sicilian Spaghetti Sauce
(makes 1 gallon)

Ingredients:

1 - 28 oz. can of San Marzano tomatoes

1 – 28 oz. of can crushed tomatoes

1 – 28 oz. can of puree tomatoes

¼ + ½ red onion, finely chopped

3 medium carrots, finely chopped

2 stalks celery, finely chopped

2 lb. hot Italian sausage (cut into 1 ½ pieces)

1 lb. ground chuck

1 lb. ground pork

1 lb. ground veal

3 tbsp. + ½ cup Lea & Perrins

½ cup red wine

½ tsp. + 1 tbsp. granulated garlic

1 tsp. + 2 tbsp. dried basil

½ tsp. + 1 tbsp. dried oregano

½ cup + 1 cup grated Parmesan cheese

¼ cup extra virgin olive oil

¼ cup breadcrumbs

3 large eggs

Salt and pepper to taste

Method:

Open all cans of tomato products. Dump into sauce pot and put on low heat. The San Marzano tomatoes need to be crushed by hand, do not use food processor.

Meatballs: In a large mixing bowl, add beef, veal, and pork. Mix up thoroughly. Add ages, 3 tbsp. of Lea & Perrins, salt and pepper to taste, breadcrumbs, ½ tsp. garlic, 1 tsp. basil, ½ tsp. oregano, ½ cup grated parmesan, ¼ red onion finely chopped. Mix thoroughly, then roll into 1 – 1 ½ oz. meatballs. Set aside. In a large skillet, add olive oil and heat. When skillet is hot, add Italian sausage to brown (you may have to break the sausage into two batches depending on the size of skillet). When browned, add tomatoes in soup pot, then brown meatballs.

Again, it may take a couple batches to brown all meatballs (note: save oil and drippings from sausage browning to brown the meatballs). Sauté celery, carrots, and onion the same way, using the same drippings. The meat drippings will infuse more flavors into veggies. When veggies are browned, add to the pot, including the drippings. Let simmer for 6 – 8 hours on low heat. Turn heat on and let sauce sit on top of stove all night. It will mellow out. In the morning, bring sauce back up to low heat. Let cook for another hour. Then add your seasoning and spices. Lastly, just before you are ready to serve, add Parmesan cheese (if you add the cheese in any earlier, it will stick to the bottom of the pot).

This is the best sauce I have ever tasted!

Old Fashion New England Clam Chowder
(makes 1 gallon)

Ingredients:

3 lb. littleneck clams (shucked) or fresh canned littleneck clams

1 qt. clam juice

4 lb. diced Idaho potatoes

2 cups chopped carrots

1 cup chopped white/Spanish onions

2 qt. heavy cream

1 qt. whole milk

½ lb. smoked bacon

1 bag oyster crackers

¼ lb.+ ¼ lb. butter

¼ lb. all-purpose flour

Add cracked pepper to taste.

**All veggies should be cut same size

Method:

In a saucepan, melt ¼ lb. butter, then add flour to make roux. Once mixture is combined, let cook for 5 – 6 minutes to cook out flour taste. Set aside. In another sauce pot (large enough to cook diced potatoes in water) take off heat when potatoes are fork tender. Wash off in colander and drain. In soup pot, brown off bacon. Leave bacon and drippings in pot and add carrots, onion, and celery to soften. Add clam juice, milk, and cream. Do not boil! You want it just under a boil. Slowly add roux to thicken (a little at a time). When thickened, add clams, potatoes, and pepper to taste. When ready to serve, drizzle a little melted butter over chowder in cup/bowl, and serve with oyster crackers.

Having grown up in New England, this is a staple of life. Some restaurants whole reputations are based on this recipe…ala the Union Ouster House in Cambridge, MA

Grandma's Baked Lasagna
(Serves 8 – 10)

Ingredients:

1 lb. regular lasagna noodles

1 lb. ground chuck

½ lb. ground port or ground Italian sausage

½ lb. ground veal

2 carrots, finely chopped

½ red onion, finely chopped

2 celery stalks, finely chopped

1 - 14 oz. Ricotta cheese

1 - 8 oz. shredded mozzarella cheese

1/8 cup + ¼ cup grated parmesan cheese

1 - 28 oz. can of San Marzano tomatoes (crushed by hand)

1 – 28 oz. crushed tomatoes

2 large eggs

1/8 cup + ¼ cup Lea & Perrins

Salt and pepper to taste

1 tbsp. + 2 tbsp. dried basil

1 tsp. + tbsp. dried oregano

1 tsp. + 1 tbsp. granulated garlic

4 oz. red wine

Method:

For meat sauce: In a large skillet, brown off chuck, pork, and veal. Put into soup pot and add cans of tomatoes. Place on low heat, (simmer). Reserve drippings in skillet, then add carrots, onion, celery, and sauté until tender. Add all (including drippings to sauce pot). Stir and let simmer for 1 – 2 hours. Season with ¼ cup Lea & Perrins, garlic, basil, wine, oregano, ¼ cup parmesan cheese, very little salt, and pepper. Let cool and set aside.

In another soup/spaghetti pot, fill with water, add salt, and bring it to a boil. Add lasagna and cook to ¾ of doneness, (it will finish cooking during baking process). It will absorb sauce better during the baking process if not fully cooked. Wash in colander with cold water to drain.

In mixing bowl, add Ricotta, 1/8 cup parmesan, 1/8 cup Lea & Perrins, pepper to taste, 2 tbsp. basil, 1 tbsp. oregano, 1 tbsp. garlic, 2 eggs and mix thoroughly.

In a large lasagna pan, put 1 ladle meat sauce and spread all over bottom of pan. Then lay 1st layer of noodles length wise in pan. Add ½" layer of Ricotta mixture over noodles. Next add another layer of noodles opposite way, then top with meat sauce. Add two more layers the same way as the first two layers. Then sprinkle entire 8 oz. bag of shredded mozzarella over top. Next sprinkle 1/8 cup grated parmesan over top. Place in preheated 350°F oven and bake for 40 – 45 minutes or until top is golden brown. Take out of oven and let cool for 10 – 15 minutes then cut into portions.

A lasagna done right is not an inexpensive dinner selection, but it is so satisfying. I usually prep the lasagna to completion the day before when doing a dinner party. The night of the dinner, I take the prepped dish out of the fridge, and put it in the oven.

Chicken Parmesan
(makes 4 servings)

Ingredients:

2 – 8 oz. chicken breasts, cut in half (4 pieces)

2 oz. Italian breadcrumbs

Egg wash (2 eggs and ¼ cup milk, beaten, mixed together)

1 cup flour

¼ stick butter

1 tsp. granulated garlic

8 oz. marinara sauce (see other recipe)

8 oz. mozzarella cheese, sliced into 1 oz. slices)

1 oz. grated Parmesan cheese

Salt and pepper to taste

Method:
Cut breasts in half, then pound out to a ¼" thick cutlets with a meat tenderizer. Set aside. Take 3 pans, one for seasoned flour (salt, pepper, granulated garlic), one for egg wash, and one for Italian breadcrumbs. First, heat skillet and melt butter. Add breaded cutlets and sauté. For 2 -3 minutes each side. Set aside to cool. Place cutlets on baking sheet, top each with 2 oz. marinara sauce then top with grated parmesan cheese, and place 2 slices of mozzarella. Put into preheated oven at 350°F and bake for 7 – 10 minutes (you only want to melt cheese and bring back to temp). Serve with your favorite pasta.

The Italian section of St. Louis is called "The Hill." You can't go wrong…when in Rome…

CHAPTER 2

California Dreamin'

After graduation, some of my friends and I drove to California for a couple weeks. We ended up staying for a year. We couldn't resist the sun and beaches. For the first couple weeks, seven of us lived in a studio apartment in Glendale. We all found jobs. The funniest one was a gravedigger's job in a "Pet Cemetery," for Mark G. Another landed a job driving a "Roach Coach" food truck. I landed the head cook position at the West Valley Hospital in Encino, California. I loved my job due to the fact that I could be as creative as I wished in feeding the doctors and staff of the hospital. Of course, I also had to follow the Dieticians rules in feeding the patients (we called them the inmates).

One day, I cut my finger with a knife, and it required a few stitches. The doctor attempted to give me a tetanus shot, but I told him I was allergic to the tetanus vaccine. He informed me it was not the serum of the old days, so I approved him to inject me. When I got home later that day, I began assembling my waterbed (very trendy at the time). I laid down to rest on the floor during the assembly and fell asleep. In the morning, I woke up and was in a lot of pain. Every joint made me feel like I was 100 years old. It took me what seemed like forever to get ready for work. I prepared breakfast, then went to my manager to tell him how I felt. He sent me to the doctor to get myself checked out. The next thing I knew, I was lying in a hospital bed for the next three days. I had a reaction to the injection. The hospital stay was completely on the house. The best part was the fact that all the nurses and aides I fed daily came to visit. One aide caught my attention and admiration. Her name was Violet. She was half Mexican and half Aztec Indian…stunning! She had hair down to the bottom of her back. We began dating. I found out she came from a close, religious family in Puebla, Mexico. She had 27 brothers and sisters. Her family owned a large plantation (they would have to, to feed a crowd like that). She was sponsored to the US by a nurse at the hospital, who happened to be married to Ron Elly (He played Tarzan on TV back in the 1970s). One day, Violet came to me and told me she was house sitting for the Elly's since Ron was filming on location and he took his wife. When I got to their home, Violet took me into their bedroom only to see a jungle looking room, complete with swinging vines. It was amazing!

Shortly after, my friend and I had tickets to see a group named Little Feet. The day of the event, I received a call from my roommate, Mark. He told me that the chef that was cooking for Little Feet took ill and asked if I would be interested in cooking for the group that night? Are you kidding? Of course! I brought Violet, got our ticket price refunded, paid on top of that, and drank all night for free with the group. Oh…Linda Rondstadt, Frank Zappa and the Beach Boys were present as well!

My birthday that year landed on Easter Sunday, so we had a big feast. My roomies made me a chocolate cake with chocolate icing. Instead of candles, they put joints…so we didn't light them. Mark told me one candle had an added surprise, not telling me what the surprise was.

Usually, I would drive to the beach after work every day. I would have to drive through one of the canyons to get to Malibu Beach. On the ride, I would light up one of my candles, crank up my stereo and drive. This one day, I followed through with my routine. I got far enough to actually see Malibu, but never reached my destination. I had to pull off the road and stop. The stereo was still blasting, my foot was on the brake, hands clutched to the steering wheel, and I stayed in that position for hours. When I finally came to my senses, the sun was going down, so I turned around and drove home. I told my roomies of my experience. Then, and only then, did they tell me what was in the loaded candle. I'll leave that up to you to decide. I went to bed and awoke at 3:30 AM to go to work. I was preparing the featured item of the day for breakfast when the phone rang. I was my roomies calling me to see if I was doing okay. I told them all was well and went back to preparing that day's feature. While I was diligently performing my task, I looked over to my left (not two feet away) and realized I had already prepared the same dish. The feeling took a couple of days to go away.

The whole year in LA, I realized that I needed to change, or I was not going to go further in my career. I moved back to the Boston area to get refocused. By this time, I had fallen in love with Violet, but was not in a financial condition to support her and make her happy. When I left LA, I promised Violet that I would get my life straight, then move her up to be with me. She waited for two years, then one day, Violet called me to inform me she couldn't wait any longer. She was going to marry someone else. It was the single largest mistake of my life. To this day, I regret my stupidity.

California
Dreamin'

Old Fashion Chicken Salad
(Serves 6 – 8)

Ingredients:

6 boneless skinless chicken breasts

4 qt. water

1 cup mayo

1 cup sour cream

2 medium dill pickles

30 red seedless grapes (cut in half)

½ cup dried cranberries

2 stalks celery, cut in ½" pieces

2 tbsp. dill pickle juice

1 tbsp. lemon juice

½ tsp. granulated garlic

½ tsp. dill weed

Salt and pepper to taste

Method:

In a soup pot, bring water to boil, add salt. Place chicken in pot. Cook for 20 minutes. Remove from pot, let cool. Cut into ½" pieces. Add celery, grapes, cranberries. Then in a mixing bowl, add the spices/seasonings, and mix. Pour over chicken mixture and mix thoroughly. Tastes better when served at room temperature.

This is good just as is, but even better with some Boston Brown bread with a dab of cream cheese.

Grilled Free-Range Chicken

Ingredient:

8 oz. boneless chicken breast (1 boneless chicken breast per person)

1 clove garlic finely chopped

2 oz. seasoned breadcrumbs

1 lemon (juiced)

Salt and pepper to taste

1 oz. olive oil

1 oz. butter

2 oz. Caribbean citrus relish

Method:

Dredge chicken breast in seasoned breadcrumbs. Place in a hot sauté pan, where the oil, butter and garlic have already cooked down. After chicken is fully cooked, add lemon juice, salt and pepper. Finally, top with citrus relish before serving.

This was a big hit in Trinidad and Granada

Di Marco Street Italian Casserole
(Serves 6)

Ingredients:

24 oz. hot Italian sausage (sliced ½")

18 oz. chicken breast meat (diced ¾" cubes)

18 oz. sweet potatoes (steamed + cut into ½" cubes) skin on

2 large green peppers (cut into 2" strips)

1 lb. Portabella Mushrooms (sliced)

1 red onion

4 oz. red wine

2 oz. Lea & Perrins Worcestershire sauce

1 ½ sweet basil

2 oz. extra virgin olive oil

Salt and pepper to taste

2 oz. grated parmesan/Romano cheese

Method:
Sauté Italian sausage, chicken breast, and sweet potato ahead of time (separately), then in a sauté pan, heat olive oil. Begin to reheat sausage and chicken, add peppers, onions, and mushrooms – cook for 10 minutes. Add potatoes last, then season with the Worcestershire sauce, bail, salt and pepper, and red wine. Ladle up on a dinner plate and top with grated cheese (serve hot with garlic bread)

Pork Tenderloin Sliders w/Fresh Dill Sauce
(makes 12 sliders)

Ingredients:

1 port tenderloin

2 tbsp. dry rub (recipe on separate page)

12 pack Hawaiian sweet rolls

1 cup fresh dill sauce (recipe on separate page)

Method:
Thoroughly rub port until 100% covered. Massage into meat. Pace into baking dish and bake in preheated oven at 350°F for 40 minutes. Dry rub will keep port very moist. Let cool. Slice Hawaiian rolls in half. Cut pork about ¼" thick and place one slice on each roll. Arrange on platter. Put dill sauce in bowl/cup and add to platter.

This recipe can also be prepared with pork loin rather than tenderloin. Obviously, it will be a bit les tender.

Scallops Wrapped In Bacon
(Serves party of 15 – 20)

Ingredients:

1 lb. Sea scallops

1 lb. Bacon, cut in half

1 can slivered almonds

1 oz. soy sauce

1 oz. white wine

1 tsp. granulated garlic

1 cup water

Toothpicks (non-colored)

Method:

Look at scallops and remove little membrane if necessary. Cut into ½" to ¾" pieces or use whole (will get more portions of you cut). In a small mixing bowl, add same number of slivered as you have scallop pieces. Place almond slivers as you have scallop pieces. Place almond slivers along with water, soy, wine, spice to mixing bowl. Let marinade for ½ hour. Lay out ½ slices of bacon in a row, place 1 piece of scallop and 1 piece of almond, place on bacon, then roll up. Secure with toothpick. Place in baking dish and put into preheated oven (350°F) and bake for 10 – 15 minutes or until bacon is cooked. Serve warm.

Another great party hors d'oeuvres. It's simple and easy to make a few hours ahead.

Shrimp & Avocado Gazpacho
(Serves 6 – 8)

Ingredients:

1 lb. 31 x 35 shrimp, peeled and deveined

2 ripe Haas avocados

1 oz. lemon juice

1 oz. lime juice

1 oz. white wine

1 tbsp. ground cumin

Salt and pepper to taste

1 tsp. dried oregano

1 tsp. dried basil

2 tbsp. Lea & Perrins

1 tsp. granulated garlic

1/8 stick butter

½ bunch chopped cilantro

1 medium jalapeno, finely chopped and seeded

½ large green or red sweet pepper, finely chopped

3 medium carrots, finely chopped

1 – 5.5 oz. can of V-8 juice

1 pint vegetable stock

2 large plum tomatoes, finely chopped

2 stalks of celery, finely chopped

¼ red onion, finely chopped

Method:

Finely chop all veggies (expect for avocado), put into large mixing bowl. Add all juices/stock/seasonings. In a skillet, melt butter, then add shrimp. Sauté 2 minutes on each side with lemon juice, garlic, wine, then let cool. Chop into ½" pieces and add to bowl. Lastly, dice up avocado (same size as shrimp) and add to bowl, mix thoroughly. Tastes best if served at room temperature.

This recipe looks difficult, but just follow directions. Finely chop all the veggies. It is so much better than putting the veggies in a food processor. It has much more texture.

Baked Halibut

Ingredients:

8 – 9 Halibut filet

2 oz. of Macadamia nuts

2 oz. margarine

1 oz. lemon juice

Salt and pepper to taste

Method:

Preheat oven to 350° Fahrenheit. In a small saucepan, melt the margarine. Ground the Macadamia nuts into the food processor. Take the filet, and dredge in the grounded Macadamia nuts until totally covered. Spoon the melted margarine covering all the top of the fish. When completed, add the lemon juice, and last, salt and pepper. Place in oven and bake for 12 – 15 minutes. You will know when it is done, it will start to flake. Pull from oven and serve.

Another New England staple. Halibut is a very white flakey fish.

Down Home Maine Lobster Salad Roll
(per person)

Ingredients:

1 ¼ lb. Maine lobster (per person)

¼ cup mayo

2 tsp. lemon juice

½ stalk celery cut into ½" pieces

Salt and pepper to taste

1 New England hot dog buns

Method:
In a soup pot, bring water to boil, add salt. Place lobster into pot and cook for 10 – 12 minutes. Remove and cool. Crack shell and remove from shell. Cut into ¾" pieces, place into mixing bowl, add mayo, lemon juice, salt (if needed) and pepper to taste. Mix thoroughly, but gently. Butter hot dog bun and brown in sauté pan. Then place salad into bun (oven stuff salad into bun).

Note: It's difficult to realize that lobster was considered inedible for most people but was served to prisoners during the 17th and 18th centuries.

CHAPTER 3

A Blizzard And Rolling Turkeys

Shortly after returning home to the Boston area, I was hired as the executive steward of the Sheraton in Boxboro, MA. This was a brand new 400 room hotel with extensive banquet facilities. I was responsible for ordering and receiving the food, liquor, supplies, and overseeing the events and the utility people in the kitchen. This included a total inventory of almost $100,000.

One of the first projects was getting ready for a prime rib dinner for 2,000 people. I had learned through experience, the slower the prime rib is cooked, the less loss you get. That was important in calculating how many lbs. of prime rib to order. These whole ribs weighted 18-22 lb. per piece. Assuming we got 20 slices of beef out of a rib, we would need to cook 100 whole 109 prime ribs. I logistics were mind boggling. I had to order the ribs, receive, and store, cook, and keep at temperature just before service. I had eight double convention ovens at my disposal. We had to cook off the ribs in shifts, then find a space to keep them warm while more were roasting.

It took two serving lines to pump out these dinners with one person using electric meat slicers at the head of the serving line. The sous chef and I were at the head of each line. The service took 34 minutes from first plate to the last. Not bad!

A few months later, winter was upon us, and the forecast was for the Boston area to get a huge snowstorm. Little did we know, what we were going to experience the blizzard I1978. The good news was I had just received all my groceries, liquor, and beer the morning of the storm. I had finished my shift before I left to go home. I asked the executive chef if he would like me to come back just in case the storm was as bas forecast. He told me to pack a few things and come back. He made arrangements for me to I a room. The first night arrived and it began to snow. By 11PM, there was 8" – 10" of snow on the ground. The whole night crew stayed over, along with the other departments. One of the cooks had a ski mobile. He made a trip to the liquor store before it closed. We had cases and kegs of beer, and liquor for our expected adventure. By the next morning, there was two feet of snow on the ground. The hotel was 100% full. We were not staffed to do ala carte service, we instead set up buffets for breakfast, lunch, and dinner. To top off this event, the National Guard was staying at the hotel with all their heavy snowplows. Did I mention that the chef and sous chef were stranded at their homes, so I was the senior person in the Food and Beverage Department? We had to be awake at 3:30 AM to setup breakfast for the National Guard so they could be on I road by 6:00 AM. The storm produced 54" of snow. We were stranded for five days. By the end of the storm, all my shelves were bare, and the bar was dry.

The hotel's restaurant had one kitchen in the dining room. One day, we had a group meeting in our banquet hall. They had no menu planned on the day of their meeting, so we prepped for a slightly larger head count for lunch. Normally, lunches were not a big deal. As the meeting broke for lunch, a thunderstorm hit the area. All 400 of the people in attendance decided to use our restaurant to avoid the weather. We had a cook's helper working the kitchen in the dining room. Chef came to me and asked if I would go out and help Stich (good name). I got to the kitchen and recalled he was in the "weeds" (overwhelmed beyond comprehension). The dining room was full, there were 40+ tickets he hadn't started, only two burgers on the grill, two orders of fries in the fryer and a bead of sweat that looked like someone had turned on a faucet on his head. I picked up all the tickets, told Stich to fill the broiler with burgers, the grill with Rubens, and began with the half case of fries in the fryer. I immediately called to the main kitchen for backup supplies of everything on the menu. Even the general manager was in the main kitchen doing prep for Stich and myself. Two hours later, we had produced 400 plus lunches, serviced 10 servers without a single complaint. After it was over, the GM and chef brought the sous chef and me into the kitchen. They congratulated us personally. The sous chef (Kenny) and I went into the bar and ordered a cold beer. As we were relaxing, the GM wondered through the bar and then disappeared. Kenny and I finished our beer and went back to work. As we entered the kitchen, chef asked us into his office. We both thought he was going to pat us on the back again, but no, chef went off on us like we had never seen before. We were yelled at for 10 minutes. Finally, chef said if we hadn't performed so spectacularly, we would have been fired. Lesson learned in capital letters, "no drinking on the job." Shortly after, the chef was let go. Kenny and I left in protest. Kitchen staff I very loyal to each other.

The adventure continues when I was hired as the executive chef of the Winchester Country Club in Winchester, MA. This was an "Old Country" club. Besides a championship golf course, they had their own curling rink. This was a great opportunity to get creative, where costs were not as important as quality. I learned to carve ice at the club. Every Wednesday, we had a luncheon for the bridge playing members. I sold them on the idea of doing charbroiled London Broil with a Bearnaise sauce. A few minutes into the luncheon, the GM came back into the kitchen and informed me that the members were complaining that the salad dressing was warm. I informed the GM that the warm salad dressing in the gravy boats were in fact Bearnaise sauce for the London Broil, (having money does not constitute sophistication…)

Let me take a minute to state that I was 26 years old as their chef, the youngest in club history, but my entire culinary team was very young. My sous chef was 20 years old; sauce man was 18, fry cook 17, and rounds cook 21.

Holidays were a highlight for this club. Thanksgiving was a time when all the members could get together and renew friendships and socialize. It was also a time for the culinary team to shine. We did just that! Of course, everything was made from scratch. The first Thanksgiving we decided to bone/roll/tie the turkeys, then roast them. It was a lot of work, but if you want to show off your team's skills, there's no other way to go. Besides, the wealthy don't care to cut around bones with their silverware. We worked through the night and were ready for service at 12 noon the next day. We had purchased tickets to see the Moody Blues concert Thanksgiving that night. More than one of us passed out from exhaustion during the concert.

New Year's Eve was the largest event of the year. I did an ice carving in colored ice, and the featured seafood buffet looked amazing.

At the very end of the buffet was one of our young cooks carving roast tenderloin of beef to compliment the crabmeat stuffed lobster and an array of smoked oysters, raw oysters, shrimp scallop scampi, escargot and on and on. About halfway through service, we noticed the uncooked shrimp and lobsters we used for garnish on the buffet were missing. Need I say more? I'm in the kitchen, ensuring all food is going out properly, when my sous chef comes back into the kitchen and tells me my young carver has sliced the palm of his hand open with the knife. This kid toughed it out. He wrapped his hand with a cloth and finished carving. Fortunately, folks in the North prefer their red meat medium rare. Not one member caught on what had happened. Immediately after service, we drove him to the ER for stitches.

My next stop was in Waltham, MA. I was hired at a company named The Seller Corporation. They did the food service for the hospitals, colleges, and school divisions. I accepted a position at a prep school in Cheshire, CT called most appropriately, the Cheshire School. As the chef/manager, I was responsible to feed the faculty and students at the school. My predecessor managed to put the budget in the hole during the first semester. There was so much food inventory, that during the first couple of months of the second semester, I bought very little.

By the end of the school year, I had managed to bring the deficit back to a breakeven point. My company and the school administration were quite relieved and happy. We were able to put a good team togethers, so I was promoted to be a member of the opening team. This was exactly what I was looking for in my career.

My first stop was to open a new restaurant in Newport, RI. What a neat place. The college's name was Salve Regina College. It was a private women's college run by nuns. My responsibilities were to setup the menus, put a solid team in place, then when the permanent general manager was hired, get him/her acquainted with the paperwork flow, schedules, inventories, etc. Every Friday, I would report to the boss. Other than that, I was on my own. The young man who was hired to take over, Ray, picked up quickly, so my boss told me to take Ray out on the town…to put on my own expense account. So, on that Saturday, we went out and for lack of better words, got blasted." At some point, I hit a median with my customized pickup truck. I managed to badly dent the doors on the driver's side, blow out both tires on the driver's side, and bent both rims. The truck wasn't drivable. A Newport cop stopped at the scene, saw how wasted we were and to me he was leaving, but when he returned, my truck and I needed to be gone. We called a tow truck. The driver gave me his card and a ride back to the Historic Hotel where I was staying. Ray was in no condition to drive, so I ordered a roll away bed for him. I passed out on my bed, but apparently Ray wanted a night cap in the hotel lounge. So, in nothing but his tighty whities, he went down to the lobby and attempted to get in the lunge that had been closed for a couple hours. The front desk called my room to inform me about the incident. I was told later that I disavowed any knowledge of knowing Ray, but the auditor saw us come in together from our "excellent adventure." Security helped Ray back to the room. The next morning, Sunday, people were going past our wide-open door, making comments about the disgusting dude in room 109. Late morning, maybe 10 am, I finally awoke with a splitting headache. I remembered bits and pieces of the night's activities. Something told me go look out the window to ensure my truck was in one piece since I wrecked it. The truck was nowhere to be found. Then I found the tow truck driver's card. I inhaled several aspirin with some coffee, then called the towing company. I reached the driver, and he was very nice. He found a couple rims and tires from the car graveyard and got my truck mobile again. He informed me I was quite abusive to him the night before, so I apologized, thanked him, and gave him a very respectful gratuity. Fortunately, he was a forgiving man and $700 later, my truck was restored to its beauty.

By Monday morning, we had fully recovered. Ray and I were called to the administration's office. All I could think was that they had heard about our activities. We were both relieved to hear that the school wanted us to put on a 50th anniversary celebration for the Mother Superior. Let me digress for a moment and describe exactly where Salve Regina College is located. The college was in and amongst the group of mansions on the "Cliff Walk." These mansions were the Summer Colleges of the Astor's, the Vanderbilt's, and the Rockefeller's. Most of the homes were built during the "Gilded Age." The 1890s. They cost $4-$5 million dollars to build in the 1890s. The main mansion of the college was donated by one of the famous elite families. As you walk into the front room, you see a 30ft wide staircase leading up to the second floor. The main dining room holds 250 people. The trim around the doorways and windows was gilded in 24 carat gold leaf. Truly amazing! All of these summer cottages overlooked the ocean.

Okay…back to reality. I decided to add some type of alcoholic spirit to each course. The first course was a half pineapple carved out. I did a fresh fruit compote that I marinated in white rum for 24 hours. After I stuffed it back into the pineapple, I sprinkled shredded coconut over the mixture. Next, for the main course, I purchased a steamship round of beef, 80 – 100 lb. of hind quarter of the critter. It was almost 4 feet tall. I carved out the marrow at the end of the leg, and placed sterno (liquid that will burn) and lit it as I wheeled it into the dining room with the lights off. We also splashed a bit of 151 proof rum for effect. The last course was five 18" to 24" Flaming Baked Alaskans. My biggest challenge was to brown the meringue. With a cake so large, I found out after the fact, it would not fit under the broiler to brown. I called the engineering department and asked for a blow torch, (this was before blow torches were a common tool in the kitchen). I then went into the walk-in freezer to do my thing with an audience of cooks and engineers. An ovation followed.

My company then sent me to the city of "Brotherly Love" …Philadelphia. My next stop was another women's college called Bryn Mawr College. It had famous alumni such as Sandra Day O'Connor. Their unspoken motto was "Our failures just get married." Please remember, this was 1979-1980, long before the "Me Too" movement. My assignment was to run one of the five dining halls on campus. I loved challenges which worked in my favor, especially since my dining hall was about 40% lesbian. It would be an understatement to say that ladies were not happy to have a male cooking for them. I made a focused effort to win them over. We began with a meeting. I asked for feedback and received it as to what menu preferences would be of interest. All the inhabitants were aware of how filthy the kitchen and dining rooms were. My team began deep cleaning, painting, and repairing. The ladies saw dramatic improvements in the sanitation and food quality. By the time I was moved to my next project, I was surprised by the going away party that was held in my honor. They gave me a bottle of Black Velvet liquor and a one-pound Hershey's Kiss. I was touched.

At Thanksgiving, I volunteered to cook the turkeys for the 800 students remaining at the school for the Holiday. My assignment was to prepare and roast approximately 30 turkeys. To accomplish this task, I was given a truck (like the UPS trucks with the roll up back door), and the use of the two kitchens with convention ovens. The project took about 12 hours, as I traveled back and forth between the two kitchens. I completed the day's work and placed the last of the cooked turkeys in the back of the truck. I forgot to roll down the back door on the truck. I stopped the truck to turn right on a hill, and a few of the turkeys fell out of the back, rolled down the hill. One turkey hit the grill of a car at the stop sign…really! The driver got out of his car, looked at his grill, (no damage) leaned down and picked off a piece of the turkey, placed it in his mouth. He said it was really good! I picked up the turkeys, placed it in the truck, and drove off. Now, I'm not saying if that turkey made it to the serving table…but…

From Bryn Mawr, I was sent to the lovely Berkshires to the town of Great Barrington, MA. The assignment required me to run the operation at an "early college." An early college was an advanced school where young adults in the 14 and 15-year-old range attended college. I was still under the age of 30 and was twice the age of some of these kids. I felt old when I overheard two of the students talking. One said in amazement that she didn't know Paul McCartney was in a band before Wings!

I was at home one day and decided to make a pot of spaghetti sauce (the Italians called it gravy). The sauce was simmering on the stove when the phone rang. It was a couple friends from Philly! They wanted me to come down for a long holiday weekend. I love the idea, so I turned the sauce off to cool and began packing for my trip. I walked right out of my apartment and left the sauce on the stove. Five days later, when I returned, I noticed my blunder. In removing the cover, I could see a small ring of mold. Tomatoes are very acidic, so I scraped the mold off and brought the temperature of the heat back to the 165°F. That would kill any harmful bacteria. Then I tasted the sauce and to my amazement, the sauce was outstanding. Possibly, the best I had ever made! To this day, my sauce is allowed to sit overnight to get mellow.

At the same time, I was working at my job with The Seiler Corporation, I started a small catering business, and I called it "The Silver Spoon" catering. We lived very close to the local snow ski area, which was a win for when season was upon us. Thousands would come up from New York City to ski. I set up a gas grill right under the main chairlift. Skiers would smell my BBQ chicken halfway up the mountain. Needless to say, business was brisk. After ski season was finished through, the 900 permanent residents could not support my business.

Community Life
Local man molds 'silver spoon'

Silver to wood

Richard Spoon, owner of the newly established "Silver Spoon" catering service at Catamount Ski Area, Hillsdale, sips a taste of his special spaghetti tomato sauce from a wooden spoon in the kitchen of his Taconic Shores home. Spoon boasts that his sauce is the best he has ever tasted, created from a blending of varied ingredients for many long, slow hours. (kc)(Register-Star photo by Kathleen Carducci)

By KATHLEEN CARDUCCI
TACONIC SHORES —

Richard A. Spoon of Taconic Shores may not have been born with a silver spoon in his mouth, but his culinary ambitions have resulted in the birth of his "Silver Spoon" catering business based at Catamount Ski Area.

Launched a month ago, the business plans to incorporate special entertainment events with a unique epicurean service. Currently, he is seeking people to employ to provide the services and news travels fast among people interested in catering.

Mawr College.

"I had a United Nations ambassador's daughter working for me in the kitchen," he said. "They were from all over the world."

Currently, Spoon also promotes employee package deals for Catamount with his roommate Dave Dollner, coordinated with concerts, bands, mountain climbing and skiing features. A luau will be presented May 2, and Spoon announced the group Shenandoah is expected to perform at the ski area Memorial Day weekend.

Silver Spoon also caters to

ROAST DUCKLING WITH ORANGE SAUCE
3 ducklings, cut in half
4 ounces orange juice
4 ounces Gatorade
2 ounces cornstarch
1 ounce lemon juice
1 tbsp. sugar
salt and pepper to taste
2 ounces white wine
Steam ducklings until about 3/4 done, or about 30 minutes. Cool.
Heat orange juice, Gatorade, lemon juice and sugar. Dissolve a small amount of water with the cornstarch and add to the juice mixture after it has reached a boil.
Add a little cornstarch at a time until the desired thickness is obtained. Add the wine and keep hot.
Salt and pepper the duck and place in a 375 degree oven until brown. Place the duck on a platter and cover with the sauce and add fresh orange slices.

ROAST TENDER HAM
8 pound smoked shoulder ham
2 ounces spicy brown mustard
2 ounces light brown sugar
1/2 ounce soy sauce
40 cloves
Pice the ham in a pot with cool water. Bring to a boil and simmer for one hour. Remove from the water and remove skin and excess fat.
Mix mustard, sugar and soy sauce and smear over ham. Stick cloves around ham approximately one inch apart.
Place in a preheated 350 degree oven for one hour. Serve with raisin sauce.

STUFFED HADDOCK
6 pieces haddock
4 ounces bread crumbs
1 ounce oil
3 ounces butter
1/2 lemon
paprika
3 eggs
4 ounces milk
Place haddock pieces in an egg wash made from egg and milk. Then place in bread crumbs.
Place into oiled pan with skin side down. Melt butter and add lemon juice. With a brush, cover the top part of the had-dock until thoroughly soaked

Food For Thought

1/2 lemon juice
1/2 cup brown sauce
12 mushrooms
Slice veal cutlets very thin into 12 2-ounce pieces and pound well.
When ready to cook, season with salt and pepper and dip in flour. Melt butter in a large skillet and brown thoroughly on both sides. When well-browned, add wine and lemon juice. Cook one minute longer.
Place meat on a platter. Add stock to the pan and scrape pan until all the residue is dissolved. Bring to a boil and pour over meat.
Serve with buttered noodles with sauteed mushroom caps. Garnish with lemon slice and parsley.

NEW ENGLAND CLAM CHOWDER
Cooked clams
2 quarts clam juice
2 quarts milk
2 pounds cooked, cubed potatoes
2 stalks celery
1 onion
3 ounces butter
3 ounces flour
2 ounces pimento
6 strips cooked and broken bacon
Mix together clams, juice, cooked unpeeled potatoes and pimento. Saute celery and onions and add to mixture.
Bring milk to a boil and add the roux of cooked flour and butter until milk is very thick. Then add to clam mixture.
Add bacon and simmer for one half hour. Add a chunk of butter and let melt just before serving.

POACHED BLUE FISH
3 pounds blue fish
1 pound carrots
1/2 pound carrots
1/2 pound onions
4 stalks celery
4 cloves garlic
2 cups soy sauce
3 ounces butter

food & recipes

Ocean's Fresh Fare Beefs Up Entrees Served To 'Merrie'

AN ANTIQUE rotisserie broils the Cheshire's prime rib. Food and Beverage Assistant Manager Richard Spoon says the restaurant has made arrangements to fly in fish fresh from the east coast daily.

By Joan Rice

A succulent cut of roast beef, a bowl of hot broth and a glass of fine wine or a tankard of ale were what the hard-working commoners of "Merrie Olde England" looked forward to after a long day of labor. The simple pleasures brought relief from the daily grind which beset most Englishmen in the 1800s.

People still like to toast each other's health and share a tasty morsel at the end of a busy day, so the esteemed restaurant of the Cheshire Inn and Lodge provides just the atmosphere for such enjoyment. Designed after an acclaimed London pub, The Cheshire Cheese, (where famous authors such as Dickens, Johnson and Thackeray spent time,) the Cheshire Inn restaurant boasts lobby furnishings as much as 300 years old.

Even the rotisserie which rotates prominently in the front of the restaurant is about 60 years old, says Richard Spoon, assistant general manager of the Cheshire Inn and Lodge food operations. To accompany these period pieces, other antiques and artifacts from the 18th and 19th centuries have been brought over from Europe.

Harkening back to this way of life, the Cheshire menu recounts the way in which the English would relax after a day of toil. "At sundown the people would repair to their hear-thsides for a warming bowl of soup followed by rich roast beef and then to the local inn or tavern for a few pints of the country's finest and a bit of song."

There is no guarantee that a guest will burst into tune after a swig of such stimulating drinks as the Buckingham, (a blend of Applejack Brandy, cranberry juice and lime juice,) or the Brighton Punch, (made with secret ingredients and "a favorite rare old Bourbon,") but the "pub" specials may uplift the spirits nonetheless. Or, guests may opt for a draught of English ale or share a carafe of choice wine.

Whatever selection is made, the atmosphere and spirits are enriched by a bill of fare featuring fresh seafood or the house specialty, prime rib. Richard Spoon, food and beverage assistant general manager, makes it his business to keep on top of menu-planning. The inn has added to its selection of fine meat entrees a steady supply of seafood flown in daily from the east coast.

Spoon, who himself hails from Boston, says that while the hours-old seafood is expensive, it has been well-received by those whose tastes run beyond beef, chicken and lamb. In the past, the Cheshire has offered a variety of fish, depending on the market: swordfish, salmon, trout, haddock, sea bass, scallops, blue-point oysters, lobster and red snapper, to name a few.

"We buy with the intent of running out," remarks Spoon, explaining that there is a distinct flavor difference between frozen fish and that only hours out of the ocean. "Freshness is very important" to the inn management, he adds, so "we try very hard all year round to bring in fresh produce," even if it means going to great lengths to obtain it. As insignificant an ingredient as salad oil is made fresh daily in the inn's kitchen, Spoon reports.

If the restaurant strives for freshness in food, it also offers a fresh flair in preparing dishes which may not be found just anywhere.

He mentions the restaurant's shrimp tempura as an unusual appetizer. It is also offered in a larger portion as an entree. Although he admits that his description of the Burgershire Soup, another item listed among the appetizers, is "a canned phrase," Spoon insists that the soup is "so thick, you can eat it with a fork." Hearty ingredients go into the popular soup: ground beef, carrots, onions, celery, diced tomatoes and barley.

Aside from those previously mentioned, main courses include Beef Wellington, Roast Duck (basted with Cointreau and honey) and Veal Medallions. Contrary to the St. Louis tradition of serving the latter in a sweet Marsala wine sauce, Spoon says the restaurant offers them with a more delicate chablis sauce with mushrooms.

Tenderloin slices marinated in burgundy are among the variety of steaks from which to choose. These, broiled over an open fire, are served with a Bernaise sauce. Other steaks include the Cheshire Strip, an eight-ounce filet mignon and London Broil.

Once a lunch item, the broil was in high demand among those who broadcast the 1982 World's Series games, Spoon reports. At the time, the restaurant was serving 200 pounds per week, he recalls.

A newcomer to to the St. Louis area in January of 1981, Spoon began work at the Cheshire the following year.

Aside from the obvious adjustments one would have to make from such a marked change in environment, Spoon says St. Louisans' dining preferences were not in keeping with his expectations. For instance, he was "surprised" to learn that quite a few midwesterners en-

41

Baked Stuff Shrimp
(4 servings)

Ingredients:

11-16 shrimp

1 cup seasoned breadcrumbs

1 large stalk celery finely diced

¼ red onions finely diced

2 large eggs

2 small bottles of clam juice or seafood stock

3 tbsp. Lea & Perrins

Salt and pepper to taste

¼ lb. melted butter

1/8 cup lemon juice

Method:

Peel and devein shrimp, leaving tails attached. Set aside. In a mixing bowl, add all ingredients except for celery and onion. Taking some of the butter, sauté celery and onions until translucent. Then add to ingredients in mixing bowl. Mixture should be moist (to be able to make into balls). If more moisture is needed, add a small additional amount of butter. In a round casserole dish, stand shrimp up, leaving body of shrimp opened up (where you will place the ball of stuffing). It is best if you use individual casserole dishes that are oven-proof. Drizzle some of the lemon juice and butter, and place in preheated 350°F oven bake for 10-12 minutes (don't overbake as shrimp will get tough). Take out of oven, and place hot casserole on a dinner plate liner.

Pan Fried Lump Crab Cakes
(makes 6 each, 6 oz. cakes)

Ingredients:

2 lb. crabmeat

1 bunch green onions

1 tsp. fresh garlic

1 red pepper minced

1 tbsp. old bay seasoning

1 tbsp. dry mustard

1 cup mayo

4 tbsp. cilantro finely chopped

1 cup panko breadcrumbs

4 oz. butter

Method:

Mix all ingredients thoroughly except for crab and butter. Then add crab trying to keep lumps of crab as whole as possible. Melt butter in a large sauté pan, then add 4 oz. crab cake patties. Brown on both sides, 3-4 minutes on each (crab is already cooked). Serve with a Remoulade sauce.

Remoulade Dipping Sauce

Ingredients:

1 cup mayo

½ cup ketchup

½ cup sour cream

¼ cup horseradish sauce

Cracked black pepper to taste

¼ cup Lea & Perrins Worcestershire Sauce

4 tbsp. lemon juice

2 tsp. paprika

Method:
Mix all ingredients thoroughly and chill. Serve on side.

Salmon Spread
(makes 1 lb.)

Ingredients:

1 lb. salmon filet (skin on)

Poaching liquid (poached salmon recipe)

2 oz ketchup

1 oz dill pickle relish

2 oz mayo

1 tsp. lemon juice

1 tsp. Lea & Perrins

½ tsp. dried dill weed

1 tbsp. horseradish sauce

Salt and pepper to taste

Method:
Bring your poaching liquid to a low boil and drop in salmon filet (make sure salmon is totally covered by liquid). Poach for 10-12 minutes or until flakey. Remove from liquid and let cool. While salmon is cooling, take a mixing bowl, and add rest of ingredients. When salmon is cool, remove skin and dark meat next to skin, then by hand mash up salmon. Add ½ the sauce and mix. Keep adding sauce until you get consistency desired (spreadable with knife). Serve with favorite crackers or warm pita bread pieces.

Philly Cheesesteak
(Serves 1)

Ingredients:

2 oz of cheese whiz

1 10" loaf of Italian bread

6-8 oz thinly sliced ribeye steak

3 oz red onions, sliced length wise

Salt and pepper to taste

1 oz extra virgin olive oil

Method:

On a flat top grill or skillet, heat olive oil and place thinly sliced ribeye to brown. Add sliced onions, and sauté. Season with salt and pepper. Take cooked meat off of grill and place into sliced loaf of bread. Then drizzle cheese wiz over meat.

I got this recipe in Philadelphia on 9th street. That's where they filmed the original Rocky movie.

Pork Fried Rice
(Serves 6-8)

Ingredients:

1 lb. mahatma long grain rice

1 lb. pork loin, diced ½" pieces

2 large eggs

12-15 snow peas, cut into ¼" pieces

½ cup baby green peas

½ cup finely chopped red pepper

1 med jalapeno, finely hopped

1 med shredded carrot

1 stalk finely sliced celery

½ red onion, thinly sliced

2-3 tbsp. soy sauce

Cracked black pepper to taste

2-3 tbsp. sesame oil

½ tsp. ground ginger

1 tsp. granulated garlic

3 qt. water

Method:

Place rice in soup pot of boiling water, salted, and cook until al dente. Rinse in colander with cold water. In a large skillet, brown off diced port, then add all veggies. Cook until just tender. Add rest of ingredients and stir thoroughly.

I used this recipe when making employee lunches in a lot of hotels. My teams always enjoyed the times I'd make Asian.

Stuffed Pork Chop
(Serves 2)

Ingredients:

2 thick (at least 1"- 1 ½ thick) pork chops, bone in

2 tbsp. feta cheese, crumbled

4 oz spinach timbale mixture (see recipe)

3 oz butter

Salt and pepper to taste

Method:
Heat skillet, and place pork chops into sear. Season both sides with salt and pepper. Sear for 4-5 minutes on each side, then remove to let cool. When cool, cut pockets in chop back to bone, and stuff with spinach mixture, and place into preheated 350°F oven. Bake for 12-14 minutes. Remove from oven and top with feta cheese, put back into oven to melt cheese. Remove from oven and serve.

Spinach Timbale
(makes 2 servings)

Ingredients:

1 10 oz package chopped spinach (frozen/thawed and drained)

2-3 tbsp. grated parmesan cheese

1 heaping tbsp. sour cream

2 tbsp. Lea & Perrins

½ stick butter

¼ cup breadcrumbs

Salt and pepper to taste

Method:
In a saucepan, place thoroughly drained spinach and melt butter. Stir, then add sour cream (do not burn sour cream). Add rest of ingredients and mix thoroughly. Maybe used as vegetable side, or to stuff in meat.

I put these recipes together for obvious reasons, but the spinach timbale can be served as the veggie for an entrée as well.

Award Winning Chili
(Serves 4-6)

Ingredients:

1 flank steak (approximately 2-2.5 lb.) diced into ½" cubes

¼ cup soy sauce

¼ cup + ¼ Lea & Perrins

¼ cup + ¼ cup red wine

1 cup water

½ tsp. + ½ tbsp. granulated garlic

Cracked black pepper

½ tbsp. + ½ tbsp. basil

1 tbsp. + 1 tbsp. cumin

1 tbsp. + 1 tbsp. Mexican oregano

1 medium jalapeno finely chopped

½ red onion finely chopped

2 stalks finely chopped celery

1 – 12oz can black beans (optional)

2 – 12 oz cans red kidney beans (optional)

1 qt. beef broth

1 pinch red pepper flakes (optional)

Method:
First dice up flank steak and marinate in bowl for 24 hours with water, soy sauce, wine, Lea & Perrins, pepper, basil, and garlic. The next day, add to soup pot to sauté, using marinade. Cook down until meat is tender. Add celery, onion, and cook until tender. Add black/red beans (with liquid in cans). Cook down. It will begin to thicken. Add broth, ¼ cup Lea & Perrins, ¼ cup red wine, ½ tsp. garlic, ½ tbsp. basil, 1 tbsp. cumin, 1 tbsp. oregano, jalapeno, salt, and pepper to taste. Add red pepper flakes at end of cooking if desired.

Completion chill has no beans so you may want to add the beans as an option.

Hearty Beef Barley Soup
(Serves 6-8)

Ingredients:

2 lb. ground beef (chick)

½ lb. pearly barley

4 carrots, med chopped ¼" pieces

1 onion, med chopped

4 stalks celery, med chopped

2 qt. beef broth

Salt and pepper to taste

1 tbsp. granulated garlic

2 oz. Lea and Perrins

4 oz. red wine

¼ lb. butter

¼ cup all-purpose flour

Method:

In a small saucepan melt butter, then add flour to make roux (thickening agent). Once mixture is combined, keep on heat to help cook out flour taste (5-6 minutes). Set aside, brown off ground beef in your soup. When meat is brown, add veggies and cook down, 5-10 minutes. Add broth and barley. Barley will act as thickening agent as it cooks. When barley is tender to taste, add roux to thicken to medium thickness (you want a thick hearty soup). If it gets too thick, just add small amount of beef broth. Season with salt, pepper, garlic, lea and Perrins, and wine. Taste, and adjust seasoning as necessary. Goes well on cold night with hot biscuits or sweet cornbread.

The first thing my chef instructor at culinary school said to the class was, "if you can't make a soup or a sauce, you can't cook." He was right. This soup is so thick that it can be served as a dinner entrée.

CHAPTER 4

Quality To Quantity To Fiasco, Back To Quality

My desire to progress led me to Springfield, MA where I landed a position with a company called Flaming Pit. Little did I know at this point, Flaming Pit would be a steppingstone to the next phase of my life. After a successful trial period at their store in Springfield, MA, I was promoted and transferred to St. Louis, MO to their Flagship restaurant called, Mr. Cribbon's Old House. I was learning all the policies/procedures of the company, the quality of the food was improving, all was going well. Thanksgiving was upon us. Apparently, the year before, one of their St. Louis restaurants had poisoned several hundred patrons on turkey day with foul giblet gravy. The VP of Operations of the company demanded all restaurants to use canned turkey gravy. I had never used canned gravy in my life and was not about to begin. We did our orders. I ordered fresh turkeys, (enough to feed 800 people). We were required then to submit our orders to the VO of Operations. She cut my turkey order in half, stating I had way over ordered (she never spent a day in the kitchen in her life). I complained, but to no avail, and was told to order frozen turkey breasts as a backup (at three times the cost of whole turkeys). Makes sense…

Thanksgiving Day arrived. We were prepped, ready, and staffed. The first 400 reservations came and went with nothing but compliments. At 2PM, we had a change of staff. We broke up the culinary staff's hours, so all could spend some time with their families. No cooks showed up for the second shift. It ended up with me on the cook's line with the restaurant manager expediting (I'm now working where 4 cooks were on first shift). Next, the turkey runs out. I was slicing frozen turkey breast in place of real turkey. It was the longest shift of my life. The compliments turned into complains (massive). I left at the end of the shift in total disgust. At home that night, I sat in the dark, thinking. The next day, I went to work. The VP of Operations was at the restaurant. Not a word was mentioned about the disaster the day before. Instead, the VP was upset that the salt and pepper shakers were not lined up properly at the tables. At the end of the lecture, I walked up to her and gave her my keys. I told her apparently; she knew how to run a kitchen better than I and walked out. That was the lowest point in my career.

Brighter days were around the corner though. I applied at a four-diamond boutique hotel/restaurant called the Cheshire Inn and Lodge in St. Louis. This inn had a rich history of quality food and table side service. On the day of my interview, there were eight people ahead of me, waiting for their turn to be interviewed. Although I was not optimistic about the odds, my brash and cocky attitude raised its head during my turn in the general manager's office. I went through my spiel, thanked the GM, and left. When I got home, I wrote a thank you letter to the GM and sent it to him. A couple days later, I received a call for a second interview. On my second visit, I was offered the job! On my first day, I asked the GM why he chose me. He explained it was due to the fact that I was the only one to write a thank you letter, and they were looking for that type of professionalism (by the way, there were 25 applicants total!).

As the restaurant manager, I was responsible for service in the four dining rooms, scheduling the servers, greeters/seaters, and bus people. It was a situation where it was best to look, listen, and approve all the policies, procedures, and techniques of four diamond service. My servers were older than I. Most were engineers at McDonald Douglas Aircraft. The service folks made so much money working 20-24 hours a week at Cheshire. They could not give up their positions, despite their high paying day jobs as engineers. Everyone worked without supervision, so I could learn quickly. We did table side Caesar salads preparation, which our guests enjoyed. There was an accordion player and violinist that went around to tables playing a variety of songs at guests' requests, so there was a certain elegance about the atmosphere. The Cheshire Inn and Lodge was a replica of the Cheshire Inn in England. We had the only full suite of Medieval Armor outside of the Smithsonian Museum in the US. The assorted artifacts of medieval weapons were all around the dining rooms (insured for $5 million dollars). We had a 100-year-old rotisserie in the lobby that roasted two whole prime ribs of beef, very slowly. It took eight hours to cook these ribs to a perfect medium rare. There was so little shrinkage, that there was no more than a serving spoon of drippings in the bottom of the drip pan.

My first encounter directly with the owner, Steven J. Apted, was when I suggested we offer fresh seafood flown in daily from Boston. I had connections from when I worked at the Country Club. The owner told me I was crazy to put seafood on the menu in a prime rib restaurant, in the heartland of "Beef Country". It was a gamble on my part. The only thing in my favor was that it was the beginning of Lent. I ordered 5-6 different offerings for each night's service, only enough to run out toward the end of the evening. I did contests with my service people to sell the "heck" out of the fish. We did Sole, entrees. Well, by Easter Sunday, the end of Lent, 30% of our dinner sales were seafood entrees. Any leftovers were offered at lunch the next day. It was a big success! One of the things I liked about Steve Apted was that he was a big enough person to admit he had been mistaken.

We also had a retail wine shop at the end of the restaurant. I knew little about wines, so I needed to educate myself. Fortunately, one of my servers was the manager of the wine shop. Two or three times a week, we would open a different bottle and sample. I had to learn what wines went with our entrees. With our new seafood entrees, we added several new wines which would complement those entrees. In the end, our list expanded to 77 wines. We had a $250,000 inventory in our wine cellar. To promote these new/old wines, we did wine tastings with the staff. Then we offered a 10% wine commission to the servers. Wine sales increased dramatically in the first month by 40%. The big test was coming up on November 15th. That was the day that Beaujolais Nouveau came onto the market in Paris, France (the new wine). Between the wine shop manager and I, we decided to do a pre-fixed dinner in the restaurant the weekend of November 15th. We offered a four-course menu with glasses of the Nouveau served, as well as the wine being used in the food preparation. It was a success, and we sold five cases of the wine, by the bottle/glass. By the fifth year of this annual event, we expanded the event to a week, selling some 50 cases of the wine. Out of 3,000 restaurants in St. Louis, we were the first to offer this promotion. Soon, other fine dining establishments began this new tradition.

Now that we had a successful tradition going well, I tried to think of more. It would be helpful to increase revenue, plus it would be something to motivate my team. Figuring that we had all of these horse carriages and buses at our disposal, we attempted to try a lunch with Santa Clause. The first Christmas we advertised our lunch in the Sunday St. Louis Post Dispatch for the next Saturday. On the following Monday, we filled up our reservations. The lunch, we offered for the children was chicken fingers, fries, and green beans with gingerbread as dessert. Then our bakery made a gingerbread house where the kids would decorate to their hearts content. We asked while taking the reservations, if it were a boy or girl so Santa could give the appropriate stocking gift. Lastly, we piled all into our "Hello Dolly carriage" (from the movie Hello Dolly), for a ride in Forest Park. We were located in the SW corner of the park. We gave the young ones hot chocolate, and for the parents we added some peppermint Schnapps (called a Girl Scout Cookie). Well, the event was a big success! The next year, we expanded the promotion to two Saturdays (approximately 100 kids). By the fifth year, we scheduled the promo every Saturday, and then two shifts on each Saturday. We totaled nearly 500 children in the end!

One tradition that began long before my arrival to Cheshire, was the Easter and Mother's Day Sunday Brunch. It was a case where we scheduled all 140 staff members to pull off this effort. We were voted the best Sunday Brunch in St. Louis for 20 years in a row. So naturally, these were the two busiest brunches of the year. On a normal Sunday, we would serve 500-550 people. My servers fought over getting scheduled due to the large number of tips they made, but on the two big Sundays, we opened up the entire restaurant. This included our room holding 250, seven banquet rooms on the second floor, and of course, the four main dining rooms on the ground level. We had whole families of 10, 20 and even 30 people. It took a total of 10 hosts and hostesses and all eight managers to make it happen. We would serve 1,400 people on those two big days each.

Thanksgiving was a labor of love. Between the hours of 12 noon and 8PM, we would knock out 800 dinners. To expedite this day's activities, we offered limited menu of just four entrees. Of course, turkey was 85% to 90% of the orders but we also offered a ham dish, prime rib of beef, and a seafood entrée. My kitchen was so organized, that we knew from prior years, exactly how many turkeys to order it took 40 gallons of giblet gravy, 25 each, 26 lb. turkeys on that day to serve our guests. The next morning, we would do a recap which included an inventory of our left ovens (which was almost zero) how many staff it took a copy of all the schedules and how many prep cooks it took to ready ourselves. Eliminating waste and leftovers was a huge help in turning the profit we desired.

Besides being voted best brunch, we were also voted one of the best overall restaurants in the city, one of the best business restaurants for lunch, one of the best wine lists, best banquet house, (we did upwards of $1,000,000 year in banquets.) In 1986, we added a salad bar for lunch. That same year, we were voted as one of the top 10 in the category. It was not your ordinary salad bar…there was a beef salad, chicken salad, smoked oysters, etc. We also made all our own salad dressings from scratch. We made a Michelob beer cheese that we placed on the tables when we delivered beverages at dinner. The beer cheese was so popular that we manufactured it and sold it in the Kroger's Grocery store.

One day, Mr. Apted asked why new promotions like this weren't thought about earlier, at a meeting in his office of the management team. After the meeting, I came to Steve, and told him that current management team lacked creative ideas. He asked me what I was saying. I told him with an assistant GM and kitchen manager over me in the chain of command, many of my ideas were shot down. He asked me what I proposed since I came from the back of the house. I suggested he combine the assistant GM and kitchen manager positions. He thought I was crazy, but I knew the kind of talent was in the kitchen. Again, he had a staff of cooks there for 25 years. They were getting bored with the "same ole, same ole." Steven thought about it for a few days before he made a decision. On one side, he owned one of the finest restaurants in the city. On the other hand, he felt the restaurant was stagnating. He had a decision…keep the status quo or go with this cocky guy who had the creativity but was an unknown quantity. He took the gamble and went with my idea of combining those positions into one. So, I became the new assistant general manager with the added responsibility of also running the kitchen. This included menu writing, taste tests for new menu items, inventories and front/back of the house training. I had no idea of how much work the combined position job entailed (there's that brash side popping its head up again, but I found out quickly!).

The results were in the Yorkshire pudding so to speak. We were able to lower the food inventory, get rid of a bunch of unneeded ingredients, bring our guest comment cards to higher scores. Food cost dropped from 38% to 33%, labor was tightened up to save 3% on those costs and began to turn a profit. Mr. Apted and I spoke daily, which was a new phenomenon. He even relinquished his quality control aspects, he tasted every entrée, soup, sauce before each lunch/dinner. Recipe cards were in front of each cook. Mystery dinners came in often and promptly reported back to him, but I didn't mind at all. In fact, it made my job easier. By now, I was comfortable in this position. The menu was changing on a regular basis. We had an extremely nice piano bar with a husband and wife playing and singing. We began doing live karaoke before it was even called karaoke!

The Summer was our busiest time of the year. We opened for dinner at 5:30 PM. We were looking for a way to promote a dinner/theater idea. During the summer, the city of St. Louis held the Municipal Opera. Acts like Bob Hope, the Beach Boys, Linda Ronstadt were some of the acts that played at the Muny. Since we were fortunate to have access to ten horse driven carriages, two double decker buses, a 1953 Rolls Royce, and a 1930 Lincoln once owned by Jimmy Walker (the former mayor of NYC). We had a great hook to get people into the restaurant. We offered dinner and a carriage/bus ride to the Muny. The only hitch was we had to serve 150-200 people ala carte and be ready to get them on the rides for their evening entertainment by 7:15 PM. This was most challenging since taking over my dual role. We opened up all four dining rooms, had 10 servers on duty, 3 hosts, and I expedited the cook's line. My Executive Assistant was one of the three hosts. Linda was great! I trusted her decision to the max. Even though all my service personal were there years longer, she had them in lock step! We knocked out $5,000 dinners in the 1 hour and 45 minutes before getting all on their respective rides. Our servers were happy. They made $200 in gratuity in less than two hours, and 7 of the 10 got to clean up and leave after that time. Did I mention we had two valet attendants parking cars? That was truly a class operation, and a lot of fun!

When the Muny was over for the evening, it was the same thing in reverse. Upon return, many opera goers would head for our piano bar for a night cap or two, and maybe sing a song with the "Piano Man." This small piano bar had about 40 seats, including the bar stools, but we did almost $1 million in liquor sales annually…amazing! This was done largely with one bartender and one cocktail server.

The King's Arm Pub, as it was known, had some famous people stop by (on regular). Like Bob Costas, the NBC Sports announcer, and Paul Newman, when he was the driver for the Budweiser Racing Team, Ted Turner, the owner of the Atlanta Braves, (he would stay at our Boutique Hotel when the Braves came to town). The first time I met Paul Newman, he spent a week at our hotel. He would come in for breakfast and dinner. I would get to work at 6:00 AM and he was jogging with two bodyguards every morning. Then he would have a breakfast of fruit, coffee, and juice. His bodyguards would not let him sign the check, they did. One evening, Mr. Newman came into the bar for some quiet time. Joe, my bar manager, was a jokester. He brough what looked like a cup of coffee over to Mr. Newman's chair. He had a spoon in the finger hole. Joe pretended to trip on the carpet by Mr. Newman, and it looked like he was going to get scaled by the hot coffee. So naturally, Mr. Newman jumped out of his chair, fearing the worst. All laughed later. Mr. Newman and his party realized it was a joke. The next morning, we received a phone call from Mr. Auggie Busch of Anheuser Busch's offices telling us if we ever pulled a stunt like that again, they would pull the entire Budweiser Racing Team from the hotel. That was truly a sobering event! Needless to say, we behave ourselves for the remainder of his stay. One Saturday night, before the race, Mr. Newman's wife Joanne Woodward came to St. Louis. They had dinner in our main dining room. Our guests were in awe, yet not a single person approached the table out of respect. For some reason, Mr. Newman began the rave in the last place, but he still won the race!

In 1982 and 1985, (I believe), the St. Louis Cardinals played in the world series, both times against their cross-state rivals, the Kansas City Royals. We were approached to prepare 1,100 box lunches for all the broadcasters at the home games for the World Series. For the first lunch, I decided to charbroil a marinated flank steak sandwich on dollar rolls with a horseradish sauce. I purchased 330 lbs. of Certified Angus beef flank. I used three new 55-gallon Rubbermaid trash cans to marinade the steak for 72 hours. The night before the first game, we began grilling the steaks over and open fire in the lobby of the restaurant. After the flank was grilled to medium rare, we let the meat cool, then sliced thinly on the bias. It took another cook and me three hours each to slice all that steak. M hand hurt for days! We prepared the lunch boxes, and by the game time, all 1,100 were ready to be served. We delivered them to Busch Stadium, up to the press boxes. I met people like Joe Garagiola (of St. Louis), Howard Cosell, Tony Kubek, and Bob Costas. Wow what a thrill! They allowed us to watch the game from the press box. Within minutes, I was passed out from exhaustion.

After the awful beginning with the Busch Racing Team, I did mend the fences with their executive offices. Mr. Busch began using one of our more intimate meeting rooms, to have his executive meetings. You could tell when he was going to have a meeting. The salespeople would go through our Budweiser inventory and check the dates on the beer (we always had fresh Bud products). One day, I received a call from his assistant (during a snowstorm). He was sending over a salmon, and wanted it prepared on a board for a party he was having at his home later that day. He sent the salmon via taxi. I was instructed not to pay the cab driver, since it was already taken care of by Mr. Busch's office. He had a successful party! Later that summer, I was invited up to his summer home in Newport, RI. When I arrived, it happened to be that the America's Cup was being held. When I arrived at his residence, he asked me if I would mind preparing an Italian Dinner for his guests. I agreed, but said I had no ingredients. Not a problem, he had his driver take me to the Italian Section of Providence to retrieve whatever I needed. The limo had a TV set inside so I could watch the Yacht race. I arrived at the store I was going to shop. Since it was a Monday, all the stores in this "Little Italy" were closed, yet the owner of this store was waiting for me. He opened the store, just for me. Upon my departure, I was asked by Mr. Busch to invite the owner to our dinner party, and I did so.

We made it back to the Busch residence, and I began preparing my gravy (Italian Spaghetti sauce!). After all was ready for my gravy to simmer, Mr. Busch invited his group of people and myself onto his Yacht to watch the American's Cup race. He instructed his cook to watch that the gravy was kept regularly stirred. Upon return, I began to prepare the white Provimi Veal, check y gravy, and get ready for serving. All the men in the group came into the oversized kitchen to check out the smells. They ripped off a piece of Italian bread, dipped it into the gravy, and marveled how great it tasted. We went through four gallons of gravy that evening among 30-35 guests, over 70 meatballs, 10 lb. of veal, and 12 lb. of hot Italian sausage.

A couple of months later, a gentleman came into the restaurant to meet and talk with my team and me.

He said he was interested in doing some award dinners for his company. I called for our banquet and catering director and his assistant catering director. We had dinner in the main dining room. He had a wonderful dinner complete with wines, then we showed him over our banquet rooms. We ended up booking dinners for 40 people and 100 people each week for a year, nice chunk of change. After the contracts were done, I asked the gentleman why he chose us. There were Marriott's and Hiltons he could have picked. He told me it was due to the quality of the food and service. Also, as a 4-diamond facility, we had a great reputation. By the way, the man was from McDonald Douglas Aircraft world headquarters in St. Louis. A few weeks went by, and I received a call from this gentleman. I asked him if there was any issues, and he said no. By all means, things were going well. In fact, they were thinking about doing something grander in nature. I asked him what he had in mind to which he responded, "something never seen in St. Louis before!". I thought about it for a second, then an idea popped out of my head. A New England clam bake complete with Maine lobsters' seaweed and clams. What I should have asked was how many people were you expecting before my mouth made a fool of me! So, I felt like an idiot when he said around 2,000 people. I exclaimed sure we can do that, no problem. Big problem! We had no facility or logistics to pull off something like this. What have I stepped into? Maybe my brashness had finally caught up with me!

64

My first concern was to find a place to handle 2,000 people plus have an area long enough to dig a pit long enough for 2,000 lobsters, corn on the cob, Idaho potatoes, clams, seaweed and fired up rocks. My first stop was to Mr. Apted's office to speak to him. He just happened to own 150 acres by the Busch wildlife sanctuary just outside of St. Louis. We drove out to see the layout. It was perfect. There was a large barn with a newly poured concrete floor. We could bring in bands for dancing in the evening. I called my seafood house in Boston. They would be able to fly out enough seaweed, 2,000 Maine lobsters and roughly 100 bushels of little neck clams. Mr. Apted had a backhoe to dig the trench which looked as long as a football field. He also owned a dump truck to bring in the necessary loads of rock for the fire pit. Next, I called my friend Mr. Busch. We needed 100 kegs of beer according to my calculations, so he ordered 2 tractor trailers with 48 kegs in each to arrive on site before noon. On the day of the event, we had our clams portioned out and onion bags, corn on the cob with butter, salt, and pepper, wrapped in foil baked potatoes cut in half lengthwise stuffed with sautéed sweet onions. Lastly, I added some suckling pigs. The day was sunny, it was warm but not too hot. Everything was cooked on time and ready to be served. Then it happened. We ran out of beer just before 8PM. I made a frantic call to Mr. Busch, and he said don't worry, another trailer's on the way. Thank you, Mr. Busch! We ended up going through 144 kegs of beer. That was roughly 8000 cups. Finally, I poured myself a glass of Jack with one ice cube. I sat in the corner and promptly forgot how much my body ached. Lesson learned, get all the facts before your mouth opens committing to a concept or idea. Just the gratuity that day was close to $25,000, (more than $1000 per banquet server!!!).

In my travels, a group of people heard about me. They invited me to fly to Nashville, TN and cook for them. They had planned to open an Italian restaurant in Nashville. I flew in the evening before. I was told I would be doing an intimate seven course dinner for four people at this private residence. When I arrived in Nashville, I met the man and was going to do the service. He informed me there was a small change in the seating arrangements. There were going to be 22 people at the dinner instead of four. This was a tactic used to see how flexible I would be in a restaurant situation. What I didn't realize until dinner started was the mayor of Nashville, as well as restaurant critics were going to be present. Also, I didn't realize I was going to be videotaped during my cooking time in the kitchen. The morning of the event, I was given 12 crisp $100 bills, a car, and direction to the grocery store. I managed to spend all the $1,200 (a hair more than $50 per person). Dinner was a at 8:00PM. I used every minute. The courses went out (all seven). At the end of dinner, I was invited to the dining room to receive a standing ovation! I was driven back to my hotel with a request to have breakfast with the investors the next morning. To my surprise, they made me an offer. I asked for 24 hours to think about it and was granted the time. When I got back to my job at Cheshire, I wrote my resignation, sent it to Mr. Apted, and within four hours I received a call from Mr. Apted. He said and I quote: "Aren't you going to give me time to make a counteroffer?" I told him what I was offered. The next day, Mr. Apted called me. He doubled my salary and gave me a 10% bonus on the monthly profit. I called the investors to decline their offer (1 was so brash. I knew I wasn't going to accept the Nashville offer). I had no intention of moving to Nashville. This was just a great experience for me to grow and see what I was capable of in my mind, and to make more money.

A year later, I did accept a position as Executive Chef at a place called Wolferman's in Kansas City, Kansas. I left my beloved Cheshire for a new adventure and set of challenges. Wolferman's was a gourmet grocery store where the wealthy of Kansas City would shop. It was humorous to see chauffer pushing shopping carts, while little old ladies would point to articles on the shelves, only to have the chauffer put the items into the carts. Besides the grocery store, Wolferman's was known for their gourmet English muffins. These muffins were 2.5-3 inches thick. As executive chef, my assignment was to make the 2nd floor balcony restaurant profitable. There are only two things you can do to make a restaurant profitable. You either increase revenues, or you lower expenses. Since the owner, Fred Wolferman, loved his culinary team (he could not let anyone go). They were way over-staffed. We decided to try opening for breakfast. This option did lower labor costs but did nothing to lower food cost. I had a lady friend who was the director of sales for the Sheraton Hotel in K.C. She also baked and designed wedding cakes as a side business. So, it was decided to start a catering business. We would use the same staff. Catering is also priced to bring food cost way down. To kick off this new concept, we went into partnership with my friend the sales director at the Sheraton hotel to do a "Business After Hours," affair with the Chamber of Commerce of Kansas City. This way we could show off our new catering concept, I had the idea of doing a Henry the Vlll feast. Since I had the beard, it was decided I would be Henry Vlll. My cooks dressed as court jesters, and my servers dressed as sassy wenches. We roasted off four each 40lb suckling pigs, smoked turkey legs, roasted veggies, and gingerbread, all items which could be consumed by hand, (there was no silverware). The guests got a bowl and napkin-that's it! We even managed to obtain Meade wine, which is made from honey. Too sweet for me. Remember, this represented food from 500 years ago. Some 400 Chamber members showed up for this spectacle, and we booked over $35,000 of catering business from this one event.

One of the chamber members of Better Business after hours happened to be the vice president of Tiffany's of Kansas City. He asked me if I'd be interested in doing a reception at his store. Actually, it was a coming out party for some of the debutants of Kansas City. What great exposure for Wolferman's catering business! Of course, I said yes. He wanted a wedding cake as the centerpiece. He offered $60 each Napoleon brandy snifters for us to use instead of plastic columns. He also loaded us a 5-carat diamond ring to be placed where the usual plastic bride and groom would normally be placed. An armed guard stood very close to the cake. Besides that, request, he left the rest up to my team and I to be creative. One of Wolferman's signature items were their gourmet chocolate chip cookies. They were huge and loaded with dark chocolate chips. I also made a fresh salmon pate. The clientele was definitely part of the upper crust of society. My team watched in amazement. We saw a guest remove a $150 China plate hanging on the wall, place a gourmet cookie on the plate then, take a knife full of salmon pate and spread it on the cookie. Realizing what she had done, she then put the plate on the buffet and walked away. What class!

I didn't know this yet, but I was about to meet my future ex-wife at Wolferman's. She was Iranian, (they claimed Persian due to the hostage situation in Iran in 1979). She worked in the bakery at Wolferman's, but technically she worked for the grocery store manager. The pastry chef and his bakers were my responsibility. The first time, we spent together, was when a group of us from the store went to a haunted house. I'm not sure how we were next to each other but each time we went by a scary stop in the haunted house she would squeeze my hand so hard I lost feeling. At the end of the evening, I asked her out to dinner, and she accepted.

My first red flag was her name in Persian: Sholeh. Sholeh means fire! I wanted a spirited woman, but not a death wish! I forgot to mention to her that our dinner date was at a steakhouse I was supposed to critique for a magazine I wrote for, (my pen name was Al-Dente.) All through dinner I was writing about the experience on paper under the table. Dinner completed; I drove Sholeh home. When we arrived at her door, I attempted to kiss her goodnight and she turned her head away. She said I didn't focus all my attention on her, and she was not happy. I promised if she would accept another date with me, I would focus my attention on her. She accepted. We dated for a couple months then decided to move in together with one rule: we would get two landline phones, one for her and one for me. We lived together for 9 months and no one at Wolferman's had any idea we lived together. In fact, we argued so much at the store that coworkers thought we didn't like each other. We finally announced we were getting married to everyone's surprise. At the same time, I received a call from Steve Apted of the Cheshire Inn. He wanted to know if I'd be interested in the general manager's position at Cheshire. I drove to St. Louis to discuss this idea and accepted the position. I drove back to Kansas City to tell my new wife and Mr. Wolferman I had taken the job. I did discuss the opportunity prior to my trip with my new bride. When we arrived in St. Louis, I introduced Sholeh to Mr. Apted. She took an instant dislike to him. Needless to say, Sholeh didn't visit me at work. Fortunately, or unfortunately, depending on your train of thought, Sholeh got 2 full time jobs, so I focused on my new general manager position.

Cheshire Inn & Lodge

* DINING IN CHESHIRE'S FINE TRADITION *

Having met with a great response, the Smorgasgarden continues Monday through Friday, 11:00 AM to 2:00 PM; Saturdays, 12:30-3:00 PM. The Smorgasgarden boasts an array of meat and seafood salads, fresh vegetable combinations, pasta salads, and fresh baked breads.

...General Manager and Chef, Dick Spoon promises inviting luncheon specials to add to the fresh fish and daily fare.

...The Calling Card drawing is held every Friday for those leaving their business card through the week. An added bonus...On December 1, 1985, we will have a grand drawing from all cards dropped off with us throughout the year. 1st Place—a weekend for two at the Cheshire Lodge; 2nd Place—a horsedrawn carriage ride for two through Forest Park; 3rd Place—dinner for two at the Cheshire Inn.

69

Cheshire Inn & Lodge

St Louis, Missouri

The style of Tudor country inns has been brought to life on the edge of St. Louis. The inn includes a pub, a baronial tavern and a restaurant as authentic as rare roast beef. Among the prides of the kitchen are Dover sole with almonds and pork chops Buckingham. A perfect accompaniment for the pork is Autumn Butternut Casserole, in which squash is transformed by the chef into a nutritious, pecan-topped side dish that is not difficult to prepare at home. It's also a great main dish for a meatless night at home.

AUTUMN BUTTERNUT CASSEROLE

3 cups mashed, cooked butternut squash
¼ cup butter
1 tablespoon brown sugar
¼ teaspoon salt
Dash of white pepper
1½ tablespoons butter
6 cups sliced unpared Jonathan apples (about 2 pounds)
¼ cup granulated sugar
1½ cups cornflakes, coarsely crushed
½ cup chopped pecans
½ cup brown sugar
2 tablespoons melted butter

Season squash with ¼ cup butter, 1 tablespoon brown sugar, ¼ teaspoon salt, and pepper. Heat 1½ tablespoons butter in a skillet; add sliced apples, sprinkle with ¼ cup sugar, cover and simmer over low heat until barely tender (about 5 minutes). Spread in a 3-quart casserole; spoon mashed squash evenly over apples. Mix cornflakes with pecans, ½ cup brown sugar and melted butter. Sprinkle over squash. Bake in a 350° oven for 15 minutes. Makes 8 servings.

Maryland Crab Cakes w/Homemade Tartar Sauce
(Makes 6 -8 cakes)

Ingredients:

2# Lump crabmeat

6-8 oz. seasoned breadcrumbs

3 oz. sweet onion finely chopped

4 oz. finely chopped celery

2 eggs

2 ea. whole lemons

1 clove garlic

1 small bottle of clam juice (4 oz.)

2 tbsp. Lea & Perrins Worcestershire sauce

Salt & Pepper to taste

2 oz. butter

Method:

Place crab meat gently into a mixing bowl, do not break pieces, leave whole. In a heated sauté pan melt the butter, then sauté the garlic, celery, and onions. Add to· mixing bowl. Then mix in another bowl all the wet ingredients, lemon juice, clam juice, Worcestershire sauce, eggs thoroughly. Add to main ingredients and mix well. When done, you may decide to sauté or bake in oven. To sauté, melt more butter in pan and cook on each side, until golden brown.

This is just downright good eating!

Fresh Tartar Sauce
(Makes about 2 cups)

Ingredients:

½ cup Mayo

½ cup sour cream

4 oz. dill relish

1 tbsp. Lea & Perrins

2 ea. whole lemons, (juiced)

1 tbsp. dried dill weed

Handful of chopped parsley

Method:

Mix all ingredients in a bowl and chill for an hour. Serve with extra lemon wedge on plate.

Caesar Salad
(Serves 1)

Ingredients:

6 oz. cut romaine

2 oz. toasted croutons

2 oz. Caesar dressings

Method:

In mixing bowl, add romaine, croutons, and dressing. Mix thoroughly and place on dinner plate.

Caesar Dressing

Ingredients:

3 egg yokes

1 tbsp. anchovy paste

Cracked black pepper to taste

3 tbsp. lemon juice

6 drops of Frank's hot sauce

¼ cup extra virgin olive oil

¾ cup grated parmesan cheese

1 tbsp. Lea & Perrins Worcestershire sauce

Method:

Crack eggs and drain off egg whites. Put yokes into mixing bowl. Add anchovy paste and mix thoroughly. Add rest of ingredients and mix. Leave at room temp. Drizzle over romaine and croutons.

Tempura Dipping Sauce

Ingredients:

24 oz. ketchup

10 oz. brown sugar

3 ea. garlic (crushed)

2 medium onions (finely chopped)

2 oz. soy sauce

1 oz. Lea & Perrins Worcestershire sauce

Method:

Mix all ingredients thoroughly in a bowl and let set for 30 minutes before serving.

Poached Salmon w/Fresh Dill Sauce
(Serves 4)

Ingredients:

2 lb. of fresh salmon filets, cut into 8 oz. portions

1 Long flat pan for poaching

1 - 2 qts. water (enough to cover salmon)

1 cup soy sauce

2 lemons each, cut in half and squeezed into liquid

2 bay leaves

1 cup white wine

2 tbsp. cracked black pepper

2 tbsp. fresh dill weed

Dill sauce Ingredients:

1 cup mayo

1 cup sour cream

1 tsp. dill weed

3 tbsp. dill pickle juice

1 tbsp. Lea & Perrins Worcestershire sauce

1 tbsp. lemon juice

Salt and pepper to taste

Method:

Pour water into poaching pan, then add all the ingredients of the poaching liquid. Bring to boil, then reduce heat to medium, place salmon fillets into liquid. Cook for 10 - 12 minutes, (salmon should get flaky). In a mixing bowl, add all the ingredients for the dill sauce and mix thoroughly. Mash up salmon with hands and mix again. Chill and serve. Serve with bagel crisps.

Use dill sauce like a dip when entertaining.

Prime Rib Hash
(Makes 8 Servings)

Ingredients:

Thaw your saved rib bones from freezer

2 Medium potatoes diced into ½" cubes

1 lg green pepper diced finely

1 stalk celery diced finely

½ red onion diced finely

¼ cup chicken stock

¼ cup beef stock

½ tsp. granulated garlic

Salt and pepper to taste

¼ cup butter

Method:

Take the thawed bones and steam for one hour, or until meat falls off bones. While bones are steaming, cook the potatoes thoroughly. In a sauté pan, melt butter, place green pepper, celery, and onion until tender. Then take meat from bones, potato, and cooked veggies, and place into blender until all is consistency of hash. Add stock and spices in a mixing bowl. Mix thoroughly, then make 1 oz. balls by hand and place on baking pan. Bake for 15 - 20 minutes until browned.

Great for brunch, breakfast, or dinner.

1,000 Island Dressing
(Makes 2 qts.)

Ingredients:

1 qt. mayonnaise

1 pt dill pickle juice

2 cups finely chopped dill pickles

1 pt Heinz ketchup

2 oz. Lea & Perrins Worcestershire

Pepper to taste

Method:

In a large mixing bowl, add all ingredients and mix thoroughly.

***Fresh is so much better than bottled dressing! Back in the 1950's, this was
served over a wedge of iceberg lettuce at any steakhouse.***

Pesto Sauce
(makes 1 cup)

Ingredients:

2 cups fresh basil

½ cup grated parmesan cheese

½ cup extra virgin olive oil

3 Tbsp. pine nuts

Salt and pepper to taste

Method:

Put all ingredients in food processor except for olive oil, salt & pepper. Turn on processor and slowly add olive oil until texture reaches a paste consistency. Season with salt & pepper. Serve.

Pesto goes well over most pastas. This is a light alternative to a heavy red sauce.

Veal Marsala
(makes 4 servings)

Ingredients:

8 pieces of veal (cut ½" thick) (prefer Provini veal)

½ cup Marsala wine

1/8 cup lemon juice

¼ cup breadcrumbs (seasoned Italian crumbs)

Salt & pepper to taste

2 Tbsp. heavy cream

¼ stick butter

2 lg eggs

½ cup milk

¼ cup seasoned flour (salt & pepper, & granulated garlic)

Method:

With a meat tenderizer, pound veal to ¼" thick. Set aside. Then set up your breading station with 3 pans. The first, put the seasoned flour salt, pepper, and garlic. In the second pan add egg wash, and the third pan, add the Italian breadcrumbs. Start by placing veal cutlets in flour then egg wash, then breadcrumbs. Preheat large skillet and sauté (2 minutes each side). Note: veal is very thin, so do not overcook). At the end of the second minute side, add wine, and lemon juice. Let cook for one minute. The flour on the breaded cutlet will act as thickening agent with the liquid. Remove cutlet and plate, topping the veal with the drippings (sauce).

This is just incredible!

Fresh Pasta Salad
(Serves 8)

Ingredients:

1 lb. spiral pasta

½ cup mayo

½ cup sour cream

Salt and pepper to taste

1 oz. dill weed

1 tbsp. granulated garlic

¼ lb. dill pickles, finely chopped

1 oz. dill pickle juice

¼ cup finely chopped carrots

¼ cup finely chopped celery

½ red onion finely chopped

¼ cup Lea & Perrins

¼ cup chopped parsley

Method:

Bring water to boil in pot and drop pasta into water. Cook until al dente. Drain, rinse in cold water. In a mixing bowl, add rest of ingredients. Then add pasta and mix thoroughly. Serve at room temperature.

I prefer to serve my salads at room temperature. They seem to keep the flavors up front.

Chicken Salad

Ingredients:

Chicken breasts (poached, then diced¾" cubes) (6 Each)

1 cup mayo

½ cup sour cream

¼ cup dill pickle juice

1 cup diced celery

2 cups red grapes (cut into halves)

2 tbsp. dill weed

Salt and pepper to taste

3 tbsp. Lea & Perrins Worcestershire sauce

Lemons (Juiced) (3 Each)

Method:

Poach off chicken breasts, then let cool. In a mixing bowl, add all other ingredients and mix thoroughly. Add cooled, diced chicken (chicken, celery and grapes should all be same size). Chill and serve.

Excellent chicken salad recipe!

Shrimp Tempura w/ Dipping Sauce
(Serves 4)

Ingredients:

1 lb.31-35 shrimp peeled and deveined

1 ½ cup all-purpose flour

1 tsp. baking powder

1 tsp. baking soda

1 each 12 oz. beer or 12 oz. carbonated water

2 qt. of your favorite cooking oil, canola oil is best

Method:

Peel and devein shrimp, leaving tail on. In a mixing bowl, add all ingredients except for cooking oil. You can use a large saucepan or deep fryer and heat oil to 350° F. Dredge shrimp into batter, and place 6 - 8 pieces into hot oil. Do not over crowd shrimp in hot oil, they will stick together. Shrimp will cook in 4 minutes. Remove shrimp and place on towel to drain. (You can keep shrimp warm by placing them into 200° F oven until all are cooked). 31 - 35 means there are 31 - 35 shrimp to a lb., so each person will get approximately 8 shrimp.

Dipping Sauce

Ingredients:

1/3 cup orange marmalade

1/3 cup catsup

3 Tbsp. soy sauce

2 Tbsp. Lea & Perrins

2 heaping Tbsp. brown sugar

4 tsp. very finely chopped shallots

½ tsp. granulated garlic

Black pepper to taste

Method:

In a mixing bowl, add all ingredients and mix thoroughly. Pour into soup cup and serve.

Can be served as an entree or as an hors d'oeuvres.

Veal Scaloppini
(Serves 2)

Ingredients:

4 veal medallions (2 per person)

1 Tbsp. all-purpose flour

1 oz. white wine

½ oz. lemon juice

1 Tbsp. capers (optional)

¼ stick butter,

2 oz. extra virgin olive oil

Salt and pepper to taste

Method:

Begin by pounding out veal to ¼" thick. Then dredge in flour. Melt butter/oil in sauté pan, med high heat. Then add floured veal, sauté 2 - 3 minutes on each side. Season with salt & pepper on each side as veal sautés. At end of cooking time add wine, lemon juice, and capers (capers optional). Remove from heat to plate and pour sauce over veal.

Being Italian, veal is my favorite meat. I use Provimi when I can get it.

Steak Butter

Ingredients:

1 tsp.+ 1 lb. butter, room temp

½ cup Lea & Perrins

1 Tbsp. minced garlic

1 Tbsp. minced thyme

1 Tbsp. salt and pepper to taste

Saran wrap

Method:

Place 1 tsp. butter in heated sauté pan, and place garlic, thyme, and basil, for 1 - 2 minutes, just to release their flavors. In meantime add rest of butter, Lea & Perrins, into a mixing bowl. Add sautéed items into mixing bowl and thoroughly mix. Taste, then add salt & pepper. Cut off a 12" piece of saran wrap and put and put butter mixture on wrap. Roll into log, and seal each end, then refrigerate. To use, cut ½" round off, and add on top of your freshly grilled steak or rib eye.

When I arrived at the Cheshire Inn & Lodge, St. Louis, MO, we needed something to bring our char-broiled steaks up to another notch (since it was mainly known as a steak house).

We also brought the quality up by buying certified Angus beef

Beef Wellington/Bearnaise Sauce
(Serves 2)

Ingredients:

6 oz. Filet Mignon (2 Each)

½ lb. chicken livers

¼ red onion

2 pcs pastry or pie dough (must be large enough to cover each filet completely)

1 oz. Mayo

1 oz. Spicy mustard

Salt and pepper to taste

1 oz. butter

Method:

First sear both filets in hot sauté pan with butter. Cook on both sides for just 2 minutes each side (rare). Let cool. In same sauté pan, add other oz. of butter, and sauté livers and sliced onions. Transfer to food processor when cooked and puree, Dump into mixing bowl, and add mustard, mayo, salt, and pepper. Should be consistency of warm peanut butter. Next, lay out pastry on dough. Place room temp fillet in middle of dough, add a Tbsp. of liver spread, then fold pastry around liver and filet. Arrange where pastry is pinched together on bottom of filet. Refrigerate for 15 minutes. Preheat oven to 350°F. Brush egg wash on outside of pastry to brown. Bake for 20 to 25 minutes. Stick thermometer into meat. Medium rare is 120°F.

This is a classic traditional recipe. We sold individuals at the Cheshire Inn. We cut out a "C" of leftover pastry for top of Wellington, then egg washed

Bearnaise Sauce

Ingredients:

3 egg yokes

1 cup clarified butter (remove milk solids by skimming them off melted butter)

1 oz. tarragon vinegar

1 tsp. dried tarragon

1 tsp. lemon juice

5 drops Frank's hot sauce

Cracked black pepper (most use white pepper, but I like to taste the pepper)

Method:

Put tarragon & vinegar into small sauté pan and reduce all moisture Set aside. In a double boiler, bring heat up slowly. You should have ½" of water in bottom pan. When water begins to simmer, put top pan with egg yolks, consistently whisking (do not stop whisking until sauce is complete). When egg yolks are warm begin drizzling clarified butter into yokes, again constantly whisking. If water gets too hot in double boiler, remove top bowl from heat. The idea is not to make scrambled eggs. As eggs slowly cook with butter, it will begin to thicken up. Add lemon juice. Hot sauce, pepper by whisking into sauce. Lastly, add reduced tarragon mixture. When done, you should have a shiny sauce, with no lumps of cooked egg. A perfect sauce will not separate. Keep on warm area on stove (not on direct heat) until ready to serve.

Roast Prime Rib of Beef/Horseradish Sauce
(Serves 6)

Ingredients:

6 lb. Prime Rib of Beef w/rack of bones (1 Each)

Salt and Pepper

6 - 8 cloves garlic

Method:

Preheat oven to 250° F. Place prime rib into roasting pan. Poke holes about 2 inches into meat with sharp knife. Place garlic cloves into holes, and sprinkle salt and pepper all over roast. Roast in oven until internal temp reaches 125° F. (Med Rare). Take out of oven and let rest for 15 minutes. With a sharp slicing knife, trim off rib bones by cutting right along bone line. Save rib bones and freeze.

Horseradish Sauce

Ingredients:

½ cup sour cream

½ cup mayo

1 tbsp. Lea & Perrins

1 heaping tbsp. horseradish sauce

Cracked black pepper

Method:

Mix all ingredients thoroughly, and chill. Sauce on side. Put rib bones in freezer until you have sufficient number to make hash.

This is a classic! Please cook at low temperature. At 250° F oven cooking time, you can save a whole portion! I don't have to mention how much an 8oz. or 10oz. portion of prime rib costs.

Marinara Sauce

Ingredients:

2 cans (28 oz. each) San Marzano tomatoes

1 can (28 oz.) tomato puree

1½ cup basil (fresh) chopped

3 cloves minced garlic

¼ each red onion

3 oz. red wine

Salt and pepper to taste

1 ½ oz. extra virgin olive oil

Method:

Heat saucepan with olive oil, then sauté onion, garlic, and basil (no longer than 3 - 4 minutes). Open cans of tomato products. San Marzano tomatoes will need to be crushed by hand. Add to sauce pot along with puree. Add red wine and cook down for 30 - 40 minutes. Very simple.

This is a basic Marinara sauce. Please use Marzano tomatoes. Yes, they are more expensive, and you must get your hands dirty crushing the whole tomatoes, but it is worth it!

Raspberry Vinaigrette
(makes pint)

Ingredients:

2 pints fresh raspberries

¼ cup wine vinegar

3 tbsp. Extra virgin olive oil

Salt and pepper to taste

2 tbsp. brown mustard

Method:
Put raspberries in food processor along with rest of ingredients. Blend until smooth liquid. Season with salt and pepper at end of procedure.

A great variation for a summer salad, especially if there is either fresh or dried fruit in it

Autumn Butternut Casserole
(Serves 8)

Ingredients:

3 cups mashed cooked butternut squash Ingredients:

¼ cup butter

1 tbsp. brown sugar

1 tbsp. salt

Dash of white pepper

1 ½ tbsp. butter

6 cups sliced unpaired Jonathan apples (about 2 lbs.)

¼ cup granulated sugar

3 cups cornflakes, coarsely crushed

½ chopped pecans

½ cup brown sugar

2 tbsp. melted butter

Method:

Season squash with ¼ cup butter, 1 tbsp. brown sugar, salt, and pepper. Heat 1 ½ tbsp. butter in a skillet. Add sliced apples, sprinkle with ¼ sugar, cover, and simmer over low heat until barely tender (about 5 minutes). Spread in a 3-quart casserole. Spoon mashed squash evenly over apples. Mix cornflakes with pecans, ½ cup brown sugar and melted butter. Sprinkle over squash. Bake in a 350°F oven for 15 minutes. Makes 8 servings.

This recipe took first place in the vegetable division cookoff at the Missouri restaurant show! Super when served during winter months.

Buffalo Wing Sauce

Ingredients:

4 tbsp. butter, melted

6 tbsp. Frank's Hot Sauce

Cracked pepper to taste

Method:

Melt butter in saucepan, then add the hot sauce and pepper. Set aside sauce. Deep fry wings for 8 -10 minutes or bake in 350°F oven for 15 minutes. Remove from fryer or oven and place in large mixing bowl. Pour wing sauce over wings and toss (serve with carrot sticks, celery and blue cheese or ranch dressing, depending on your taste). I prefer ranch, due to the fact it has no "carbs," and tastes better when making a hot chicken breast sandwich (recipe located on another page).

One of my favorite appetizers or hors d'oeuvres are hot wings. It's simple, but tasty!

Crabmeat Stuffed Filet Of Sole Florentine/Hollandaise Sauce
(Serves 4)

Ingredients:

6 oz. sole filets (4 each)

8 oz. lump crabmeat

1 stalk celery, finely chopped

3 tbsp. red onion, finely chopped 4 oz. breadcrumbs

7 oz bottle clam juice (1 each)

1 large egg (1 Each)

4 oz chopped frozen spinach (drained completely)

Salt and pepper to taste

1 tbsp. Lea & Perrins

2 tbsp. lemon juice

1 oz. grated parmesan cheese

6 oz. - 8 oz. Hollandaise sauce (see recipe on other page)

1 oz. butter

Sprinkle paprika

Method:

In a mixing bowl, add crabmeat, breadcrumbs, breadcrumbs, beaten egg, chopped celery and onion (that was sautéed in butter until softened). Add clam juice, spinach, lemon juice, and Lea & Perrins. Mix thoroughly but gently, so not to break up crabmeat. Lay out sole filets and put equal amounts of stuffing on each filet. Roll up, keeping stuffing inside of filet. Place into a baking dish, sprinkle paprika over filet and bake in a preheated 350°F oven for 8 -10 minutes. Note: filet is very delicate, so handle with care. Remove from oven, and plate. Let cool for a couple minutes before topping with Hollandaise sauce. If sole is too hot, it will break sauce. See recipe for sauce.

Italians do wonderful things with seafood, and this is a great example

CHAPTER 5

Knoxville, TN

My lovely bride was not a fan of St. Louis and she let me know at every opportunity, so I began looking for a new position. I received a call from a hotel company located in Memphis called Cooper Hotel Company. They owned a hotel in St Charles, MO about 20 or 30 minutes outside of St. Louis. I was set up for an interview with the general manager. The job I was interviewing for would have me located in Knoxville, TN. After my interview I didn't hear from him for a few days. I figured nothing ventured nothing gained. About a week went by, then I received a call from a man named Michael Gibson, the general manager of the Holiday Inn on the World's Fair site of 1982. We talked for a few minutes, then he asked me if I'd be interested in seeing the hotel. It sounded interesting. This was a corporate hotel in a downtown market with a mostly business clientele. I flew down to Knoxville and was picked up by the hotel van. I checked into the hotel around 10:00 AM. A few minutes later, Mr. Gibson called and said hello. He had a meeting to go to, so we would meet later. Well, about 4:00 PM comes around, the phone rings again. It's Mr. Gibson. He said to meet him in the lounge. I met him in the lounge. He asked me if I'd like a beer. Very hesitantly, I accepted. Some interviews, they watch to see if you drink and how much. As we finished the beer, he asked me if I enjoyed college basketball. He had courtside tickets. I really wasn't a fan, but I said sure, so we went to the game. We got back to the hotel around 10:00 PM.

The next morning, I had to catch my flight back to St. Louis before he got into the hotel, so I left without speaking to him. It snowed that night and there was several inches of slush on the road. The van driver was so busy talking to me, he forgot he was driving on slippery roads. Sure, enough we rear ended a car on the way to the airport.

Three or four days go by, no phone call. Then on the 5th day, Mr. Gibson called to offer me the job of Food and Beverage Director. I accepted. I came down about a month before my wife, figuring that I was going to be focused on my new job anyways.

I lived at the hotel until my wife's arrival. The first night with her in Knoxville was not uneventful. We had placed all her gold jewelry in a safe deposit box. We decided to go out to dinner so she could see some of what Knoxville had to offer. She asked me to go down and pick out some of her jewelry for the evening. I did my husbandly duty and fetched the pieces she requested. The next morning, I was scheduled to be manager on duty, so I promptly arrived at the front desk only to find out that the safety deposit box with all my wife's jewelry had been left out all night. There was in the neighborhood of 550,000 of jewelry in that box. I held my temper until the next morning and told Mr. Gibson of the situation. Fortunately, nothing was missing, but I never saw that guest service manager again found out quickly that Mr. Gibson was very detailed person, very structured. He had spent many years working for Holiday Inn Corporate. This particular hotel was a franchise property, We had a good working relationship. When Mr. Gibson worked at Holiday Corp, he was a Corporate Food and Beverage Director. We came from similar backgrounds.

I found out how to run a business from his guidance and mentoring. He taught me how to do budgets business plans as well as the aspects of running a business He expected his managers to do more and better than the other general managers with corporate hotels.

With Cooper Hotels, he had a great sales department, and the executive housekeeper was a retired RN. She was very tough on her housekeepers. The bell captain put together a great team of bellmen and Mr. Gibson's executive assistant was like a mother to all of us. The only weak link in this group was my department, Food and Beverage.

I called a meeting of the entire Food and Beverage team to let them know that 9 out of 10 complaints in our hotel came from our department. The other department guest service scores could have easily qualified for a "Torchbearer Award" if it weren't for my department. The "Torchbearer Award" is given to the top 5% of Holiday Inns in the USA. In the meeting we all agreed we would work toward qualifying the hotel for the award. That began with training, training, then more training. We also handled guest issues promptly, so guests were happy. If your guest perceives you as concerned and trying to resolve an issue, they will accept your offer and reward you with great scores. Over the next 12 months we accomplished our goal. We went a whole year without a single complaint in our own department! The second year we had but one guest complaint. The hotel qualified and won the "Torchbearer Award"! Although I was a FBD director, Mr. Gibson had me sign up to be in the General Manager Certification program. Now I'm in strange waters for sure. I was the only FB in the General Manager program out of 42 attendees. I spent 2 weeks at Holiday Inn University in Olive Branch, Mississippi. We were given 6 months of homework added to our normal workload. One of the tasks was to design a training program for your hotel. I came up with a service manual for restaurant service. Apparently, the instructors liked it so much that they made it part of the FBD certification program. After 6 months we all went back to the university to complete the program. On the last day of class, we took a final exam. Little did I know how different this exam would be. In fact, half of the class failed. I couldn't imagine going home and attempt to explain why ownership just spent some $5,000 and you fail to the course. Thankfully I passed.

So now I am a certified general manager, and our hotel has just won the highest award Holiday Inn offers. I can now take over a hotel of my own! Not so fast, there is so much more. First, we needed to get others certified in their respective areas. I had to learn life and safety standards since I was involved in all inspections

In the meantime, there was the day-to-day business. The hotel was connected to a 200,000 sqft. convention center. The next event coming in was a banquet for wide receiver for the Chicago Bears, Willy Gault. This was a prime rib party for 1,600 people. My team had to prepare 80 to 100 prime ribs, We set up to serving lines. I used a meat slicer to cut the prime ribs quickly as my chef was at the head of the other serving line. From the time we began plating to the finish, everyone was served, and it took 28 minutes. That's quick in anyone's book My best memory though was when I received a call from the baseball coach of the University of Tennessee Baseball team. The head coach was once a pitching coach for the New York Yankees...my team! The coach told me they had convinced Don Mattingly, the Yankee first baseman, to come. He was only charging the University $50,000 to do a one hour heading clinic in the basketball area. They were planning to put Don up at our hotel. I naturally put him up on the penthouse level. I had a special fruit and cheese platter put together along with a super bottle of wine. We had three lovely U.T. Coeds who worked on our service on the penthouse level. I also asked my personal executive assistant to arrange to take Mr. Mattingly down to the entertainment area of Knoxville along with my three club level hostesses.

The next morning, I met with my assistant to ensure Mr. Mattingly had a good time. Apparently, he did. He told the Tennessee coaches that he travels 7 months out of the year for away games and he was very impressed with the level and quality of our service! The coach was so taken aback that he wrote a wonderful letter of thanks. The head coach then called me personally to thank me. He asked if I like to go to New York City? I said I do from time to time. Coach then said you let me know the next time you go to New York, and I will get you tickets to see a game and get you into the clubhouse and meet the rest of the team. I thought died and went to heaven. Of course, I went to New York!

In an effort to think of new promotions, we came up with an idea for our lounge at lunch. Besides our corporate business and big game football weekends we wanted to attempt to get downtown workers to use our food and beverage facilities. We were fortunate to have some airlines contractors to stay at our hotel. Mr. Gibson negotiated with the airlines to trade 2 airline tickets to Hawaii for complementary room nights. We ran a luau promotion for five Mondays in a row. We had contests that flavored a tropical theme like a hula hoop contest, wine cooler races, and if there was a tie in a contest, we had a "suck-off." It consisted of taking a screw top of a beer and a straw. One of the contestants would screw the top and stick their straws in the bottle and suck the beer out of the bottle. Whoever finished the beer first tipped the bottle upside down and put it over their head. If nothing came out, they were the winner. We offered food during the nightly event. The main attraction was a 40 lb. suckling pig. Each week as we approached the finals, we had to cook a larger pig. By the night of the finals, we had to slow cook a 300lb. Hog. It took my cooks 12 hours to cook the hot on a large grill outside in the parking lot. When my cooks presented the hog, they paraded it around the lounge wearing grass skirts and war paint all over their bodies. Our cocktail servers and bartenders were in bikinis with grass skirts. It was very cool. On the final night of the finals there were so many people in the lounge they were packed in like sardines. We did over $4,000 and liquor that evening.

Tennessee fans were second to none when it came to game day. The big day was Saturday. I had four servers, two bussers, a cashier and seating person. I ran food for the breakfast buffet. We did approximately 600 breakfasts. We all got a workout especially since one of my servers was 65 years old and one was 70. From 7:00 AM to 11:30 AM we did $3,000 and breakfasts. When everyone was gone it so quiet you could hear yourself think again. The large lobby held 2,000 people. We decided to set up portable bars. I had the bright idea of buying the little airline bottles that people would place in their pockets for the game. We set up two portable bars. They did almost $1,000 an hour. That was a big success! Everyone clocked out after cleaning up at 12:00 noon. The game let out 4:30 PM. The lounge reopened. Bar sales averaged that evening almost $7,000. The only busier weekends were when we housed a team that was playing Tennessee that weekend. I remember when Alabama was in Knoxville, There were 116 players plus coaches and various other members. The meals were selected by team dietitians and coaches. They loaded up on carbs and lean proteins and the menus reflected such. For dinner they had pasta, baked chicken, baked potatoes, salads, fruit, green vegetables and gallons of water and iced tea- no soda. They could go back as many times as they wish to two places at a time. That was at 5:30 PM. At 8:30 PM, each player had a snack. One large cheese pizza each, 45 lbs. of baked lasagna and 15 gallons of ice cream plus all the toppings at the ice cream bar. In the morning, my cooks arrived at 4:00 AM to begin making breakfast for 8:00 AM. We prepared approximately 500 pancakes from scratch an 8oz New York strip steak, 120 lbs. of bacon, 120lbs home fries, almost 120 doz. eggs, 50 loaves of bread for toast, 40 gallons of fresh orange juice, and gallons of water- no coffee. I happen to be at the front desk to pay my respects to the coach. He was very happy. Then he handed a check for $27,000. Not bad revenue for 18 hours of the hotel. At the time I worked at this hotel, I did not get to see one game. I did get to meet Peyton Manning while he was the quarterback at Tennessee. Neyland Stadium was the third largest college football stadiums in the U.S., at 107,000 seats. Only Michigan and UCLA were larger.

Needless to say, I was putting in a lot of hours at the hotel. My lovely bride decided she wanted to earn more money, so she worked hard at the Hilton by the airport and was rewarded with a promotion to food and beverage director at the company's hotel in Oak Ridge, TN. Sholeh was working equally long hours but in the evening. If we were lucky, we would have one day off together a month. Somehow that wasn't quite enough in my book. I finally flat out told her I was lonely. All she could do was laugh. Deep down inside she was hurt, and she got angry. One night she woke me up and asked me if I remembered the argument, we had a month ago? I said no I don't remember. She informed me I needed to sleep

on my stomach, or she would cut a certain appendage off. I tried to go back to sleep but to no avail. I got up, dressed, and packed a few clothes and toiletries and went to the hotel. The next morning Sholeh called my hotel. Mr. Gibson and I were in the chef's office chatting about an upcoming event. The phone rang in the chef's office, and he gave me the phone saying it's your wife. Sholeh was screaming. Mr. Gibson took the phone from me to try to calm her down. He spoke two words to Sholeh and went quiet. He lost all the color in his face. He hung the phone up and just looked at me. I asked him what happened. Mr. Gibson said Sholeh threatened to kill him. He said he never wanted to speak to her again. In Sholeh's words

Gibson was a bad influence on me. What she didn't realize, is that she had it backwards and I was the bad influence. Shortly after I filed for divorce

In the meantime, I landed a position with Holiday Inn Corporation in Livermore, CA. My responsibilities included running the operation while the hotel changed from a corporate owned hotel to a franchise property. I didn't remember what year it was, but I do remember the earthquake that knocked out the power at the World Series in Oakland. It shook the hotel violently, breaking every bottle and glass in the lounge. Of course, at that very moment I was talking to my now ex on the phone. If you haven't figured it out, we were still in love just couldn't live together. Upon completing my task on the West coast moved back into an apartment outside of Nashville, TN. All was fine until Sholeh decided 60 hours a week was not enough to work, and she took on a part time job. This time it was over. I sold my furniture and moved to Vero Beach, FL. A friend got me in touch with a gentleman who owned a condo right on the beach. Really? Needless to say, I bought it.

The next item on my list was to get a job. Within a day I acquired the FBD position at the Holiday Inn beachside. It had just finished a hefty renovation, but the nightclub and restaurant were dead. Things were finally into place. Being a typical Holiday Inn restaurant, we did our six dinners in the evening with their typical Holiday Inn menu. Knowing that dinner should be priced no higher than 25% off the cost of a guest room. This is 1990 so at $60.00 a night for a guest room, the most expensive dinner items should be around $15. 1 came up with an Italian menu all priced at less than $15. Business picked up significantly! At the same time, we had a small bar with about 20 tables and chairs. We began doing some hors 'devours, like steak which included mini potatoes sliced top round of beef with horseradish sauce. We had an acoustic guitar player. We increased our beverage revenue from $40 to $50 per night to $600 to $700 per night. Next, we offered a seafood buffet on Friday evening and a prime rib buffet on Saturday night from $10 plus tax and tip. About a month into the promotion, we were doing $3,000 dinners each night. Suddenly, we were making money.

Fortunately for us the public building which housed the restaurant and nightclub were not attached to the hotel. Like I stated we had a nightclub, and it was closed. It held 215 people according to the fire code, so it was a good size. I began my visiting other bars and nightclubs in the coast. I would sit at the bar in each place and watch the bartender. First and foremost, I wanted to make sure all revenue was going in the register, not into pockets. Then I would calculate how much each bartender would do in sales per hour. I was looking for approximately

$500 an hour for each, there were opportunities to give the bartender a little grief just to see how they handled stressful situations. When they passed all these hurdles I gave them my business card, telling them what we were doing and invite them to the hotel. It was amazing to see their response! Then I did the same interview process for the cocktail servers. In the meantime, I was interviewing some good dance bands. I found some good deals on the bands from the Tampa and St. Pete area. I had a good DJ that could keep the crowd's attention and energy level when the bands were on break. Next, I needed a doorman. I called my beer suppliers and asked if any drivers were looking for part time door and security positions. The Budweiser sales representative sent over this guy that looked like a brick wall. I saw him pick up a full keg of beer with one hand I hired him. Their instructions were simple- take any issues outside and protect our team especially the bar manager. She was a 5' woman with fiery red hair but no match for a drunk cowboy. In 5 years, we had two issues. We didn't want the reputation for fights- it would scare a lot of people away,

Last, but not least, I purchased a custom-made blackjack table but first I checked with the state Attorney General's office for permission to use it for entertainment purposes. The Attorney General wrote a letter that we framed and posted behind the table. Guests would pay $5, get some chips and play blackjack until they ran out. The table cost us $3,000. Our return on investment took one month! I hired a young lady to deal. She was all but 18 years old. The bartenders wore black pants and Hawaiian shirts The cocktail servers wore a sleeveless tux shirt, teal cummerbunds. My 2 servers were 5' 10" each. They made enormous money. By the end of the second month, we were approaching $100,000 a month in beverage sales. Food was served until 10:00 PM. The lounge closed at 1:00 AM. My staff wasn't advised, but we had undercover sheriff's deputies keeping an eye out for drugs, etc. We were voted the best nightclub on the Treasure Coast!

Then the owner hit us with a new challenge. He owned a beat up and rundown property about 2 blocks up the road, again right on the beach. He wanted to reopen this 72-seat restaurant with a small 20 seat lounge. The menu was almost exclusively seafood since we could get fresh fish daily. We made our own bread and honey butter and made the desserts and salad dressings from scratch for both kitchens Everything was going well until we hit the fall slow season. We ended up closing the free-standing restaurant and consolidated the staffs into one
Just before Easter the next year my Assistant Banquet Coordinator set up a dance in our ballroom but neglected to write it down or tell anyone. They showed up to set up themselves and of course nothing was ready for them. About 7:00 PM I received a call at home informing me of the situation. I rushed back to the hotel. I

found a couple of people to work the function. Luckily there was a bar set up only, no food I'm pulling the portable bar across the room and the wheels get hung up on the carpet while I was pulling. (Note: Never pull always push heavy loads. Management 101.) All of a sudden, I heard a pop in my back and went down to my knees in serious pain. I was done for the evening. I went home and laid on the floor, The next morning I was in pain but not as bad as the night before.

The next day was Easter Sunday. I felt better. Now, 2 days from my accident. We are getting ready for Easter Sunday, a big day! I'm carrying a narrow 4' mirror filled with fruit and cheese. Suddenly a sharp pain radiated from my back to my hips down my legs. I was not able to feel my legs and collapsed. Luckily my restaurant manager was standing next to me. He caught the mirror as I went to the floor. He prevented further injury to me lying in broken glass if he wasn't standing there. I went home, laid down and went to the doctor the next morning, I had a herniated disk right at my belt line. I was on my workers compensation. Remember my ex-wife? Guess who came to Florida to help me rehabilitate my back- that's right. Sholeh stayed for about 2 weeks until we began arguing again so we agreed she'd leave. These 2-week visits became regular. In fact, one time she invited her mother and half-sister for a visit. In the 6 years of marriage, I had never met her mother or father, so I met my ex-mother-in-law after the divorce. Her mother spoke Persian and French, and her half-sister spoke broken Persian and French and Sholeh spoke English, almost no French and Persian. I was confused. Sholeh's mother was a pharmacist. She was very nice. I asked her one day how she was so even tempered and nice, and why Sholeh had such a temper and why she was so mean? Sholeh punched me. Her mother asked Sholeh why she hit me (I never did find out what she said to her mother) Her mother just gave me that understanding look. I was on workers comp seven months. During that time heard through the Grapevine that the owner had electrocuted himself, as well as a dishwasher, while they were wheeling out a small sailboat out to the street using the sail to advertise.

Apparently, he got too close to the power lines and that was the last thing he did on this earth. He left three daughters in charge of the hotel. One daughter knew the combination to the safe. She would make withdrawals but never deposits. Most of the withdrawals ended up on the bar top in the lounge in the form of cocaine lines.

Stuffed Pork Chops w/ Sautéed Apples & Stuffing
(Serves 8)

Ingredients:

½" thick bone-in chop, or boneless chop per person. (8 Each)

5 med. GaIa Apples diced ½" slices

¼ cup brown sugar

1/6 lb. butter

1 tbsp. ground cinnamon

1 tsp. ground nutmeg

1 oz. white wine

½ loaf white bread

½ tbsp. sage

2 tbsp. poultry seasoning

Salt and Pepper to taste

2 large eggs

1 cup chicken stock

2 tbsp. Lea + Perrins Worcestershire sauce

Method:

Sear pork chops in butter with salt and pepper, then let cool. In another saut6 pan, add butter then begin saut6ing apples, while adding cinnamon, nutmeg, and brown sugar until they are al dente. In a mixing bowl, add bread (pull it apart into one-inch pieces) with eggs, sage, poultry seasoning, Lea + Perrins Worcestershire sauce, salt and pepper, and chicken stock, Pour into baking dish, and make even with a serving spoon, then add the apple mixture. Make sure they are leveled out. Then top off with the pork chops laying side by side. Bake in a preheated 350° F oven for 30 minutes. Serve in baking dish.

This is a dish that can be prepped one day, then baked the next. It has sweet, savory, and all you need is a veggie to make it a complete meal.

Pan Fried Pork Chops
(Serves 4)

Ingredients:

4 pork chops

2 oz. of Italian seasoned breadcrumbs

2 oz. margarine

2 oz. extra virgin olive oil

1 tsp. minced garlic

Salt & pepper to taste

Method:

In a frying pan, heat oil and margarine. While that is heating place breadcrumbs in a dish and add pork chops. Cover the pork with the breadcrumbs, then place in the heated pan. Add the garlic and turn the heat down to medium. Salt & pepper as it cooks. Fry on both sides until golden brown on both sides, 4 to 5 minutes on each side. Then serve.

Goes well with oven brown sweet potatoes

Dilled Burgundy Sauce

Ingredients:

3 oz. butter

3 oz. flour

2 oz. Reg Burgundy Wine

1.5 oz. Dill Pickle Juice

Pepper to taste

2 qt. beef stock

Method:

In a small saucepan, melt butter, then mix into flour. To make a roux. (A roux is a thickening agent for sauces). In another saucepan, (at least 2 qt.) place beef stock, on high heat. When it comes to boil, reduce heat to med. Stir in roux a little at a time. It will thicken rapidly after it begins to thicken. Get to medium thickness (coating a spoon). Then pour over rolled beef in baking pan.

Beef Rouladen / Dilled Merlot Sauce (Stuffed Beef)
(Serves 4)

Ingredients

8 thinly sliced cuts of cooked Roast beef (1/8" thick)

¼ cup Italian breadcrumbs

2 large eggs

1 stalk celery, very finely chopped

½ red onion, very finely chopped

½ lb. bacon, finely chopped

2 oz. honey ham, finely chopped

1 large dill pickle finely chopped

3 tbsp. + ½ cup dill pickle juice

¼ cup red wine

1 qt. beef stock

2 tbsp. + 3 tbsp. Lea & Perrins

Black Pepper to taste

3 tbsp. + ½ lb. butter

½ lb. flour (all purpose)

Method:

In a mixing bowl, add breadcrumbs, eggs, cooked bacon bits (save drippings). In a skillet that you cooked the bacon in, add ham, celery, onions, pickles, sauté until veggies are translucent, and then add mixture to breadcrumbs, including bacon drippings. Add ½ cup pickle juice, Lea & Perrins, and mix (should be moist enough to hold together. Lay out roast beef and put 1 tbsp. stuffing mixture onto each piece of beef. Roll up like a cigar and place into baking pan (2 rows). In a separate saucepan, add beef stock to get hot. In a small saucepan, melt butter then whip in flour into a thick paste. When stock begins to boil, reduce heat to medium from high. Stir in the roux a little at a time until stock begins to thicken. Do not leave stove during this procedure. You want to keep stirring with a wire whip constantly to get no lumps. Add 2 tbsp. Lea & Perrins, 3 tbsp. pickle juice, and ¼ cup red wine. Continue stirring, taste, then add salt and pepper. When wine sauce is ready, pour over rolled beef in baking dish. Cover in foil and stick into preheated 350° F oven for 30 minutes. Serve two of the rolled beef per person, adding some of the wine sauce just before serving.

Sautéed Red Cabbage
(Serves 4- 6)

Ingredients:

1 small head red cabbage

1/6 red onion sliced in strips

2 red delicious apples, diced coarsely

¼ cup brown sugar

5 oz. red wine

1 tbsp. ground cinnamon

1 tbsp. ground nutmeg

Salt and pepper to taste

¼ lb. butter

1 tsp. allspice

Method:

Melt butter in heated soup pot. Add cabbage, red onion, and apples. Sauté for 10 minutes, then add rest of ingredients, except for salt and pepper. Let it cool down for an hour, add wine, water if needed. Cabbage will be tender when done. Taste, then add salt and pepper.

The flavors in this cabbage dish are both savory and sweet. A great compliment to the Beef Rouladen.

Basic Hummus Dip
(Makes Almost 1 lb.)

Ingredients:

12 oz. can chickpeas (garbanzo beans) drained into food processor (1 Each)

1 ½ tbsp. Tahini paste

Salt and pepper to taste

Juice of 1 lemon

Method:

Add all ingredients to food processor and mix thoroughly. Taste and add salt, pepper, and lemon juice as necessary. Mixture should stay on spoon if turned upside down. Chill and serve with warm pita bread, or carrot and celery sticks.

Hummus is very popular these days. I guarantee you will love it.

BBQ Boston Butt
(Serves 12)

Ingredients:

5 - 6 lb. Boston Butt

Dry Rub (Found on separate page)

1 ½ qt. cider vinegar

Method:

Preheat oven to 450° F. Take dry rub and cover entire piece of park. Roast in oven for I hour at 450° F. Remove from oven, add cider vinegar to bottom of roasting pan. Lower oven temp to 225° F, cover roasting pan with foil (seal very tightly to ensure no steam escapes). Slow cook for 8 - 10 hours, or until meat literally falls of bone. Using 2 forks, pull meat apart. Leave in juices. BBQ sauce is optional, not recommended.

You can't go wrong with this recipe. The rub is a Memphis rub, and the addition of vinegar is an East Carolina version of BBQ

Zesty Coleslaw
(Serves 6)

Ingredients:

1 bag shredded cabbage, with shredded carrots and red cabbage

½ cup cider vinegar

½ cup mayo

4 tsp. sugar

Salt and pepper to taste

Method:

In a mixing bowl add vinegar, mayo, sugar, and salt & pepper. Mix thoroughly. Pour over cabbage and mix. Chill and serve.

*Note: I use 4 packages of Splenda to lower carbs.

Great BBQ must have side dish. This adds a zing with any kind of pork.

BBQ Dry Rub

Ingredients:

1 oz. Black Pepper corns

1 oz. sea salt

I tbsp. red pepper flakes

1 tbsp. ground cinnamon

2 tsp. Ground nutmeg

1 oz. Hershey's Cocoa Powder

1 oz. granulated garlic

1 oz. dried oregano

1 oz. dried basil

1 oz. ground cumin

½ oz. ground ginger

1 oz. dried mustard

Splenda packets (8 Each) or 2 oz. granulated sugar

Method:

Using a coffee grinder, grind all above spices. Dump into mixing bowl and thoroughly mix. Put into container that tightly seals, and store in cabinet. When ready to use, rub generously over meat (pork, beef, or chicken) and roast in oven. If making BBQ pork shoulder/butt, follow recipe on other page.

This recipe will be more than enough for a Boston Butt (pork). You can store this rub in a cool/dry cabinet for a couple months. Works well on chicken too.

Beyond Baked Beans
(Serves 3 – 4)

Ingredients:

12 oz. can B & M bakes beans (1 Each)

Strips hickory bacon (4 Each)

2 oz. brown sugar

1 oz. balsamic vinegar

½ red onion, sliced lengthwise

Cracked black pepper

Method:

Brown bacon until crisp, removed to drain. Save drippings. Add sliced red onion to drippings and sauté until tender. In a saucepan, dump in can of baked beans, add saut6ed onions (including bacon drippings). Bring up to medium heat. Chop bacon and add to beans, sugar, balsamic, pepper. Take off heat and serve.

This is also a great accompaniment to great BBQ. The balsamic vinegar adds something I have never tasted in another baked bean side.

Roast Pork Loin
(Serves 4)

Ingredients:

2 lbs. pork loin (whole)

Salt & pepper to taste

3 to 4 slices of bacon (optional)

1 tsp. minced garlic

4 cloves of garlic

Method:

Preheat oven to 350° F. In a roasting pan, place pork roast in bottom, then with a knife, poke a few holes into meat. Place the garlic into the holes, use your finger to push it into the meat. Put salt, pepper, and minced garlic over top of meat, (use less salt if you are using bacon). Lay slices of bacon over top of roast, then place into the oven. Roast for 1 to 1.5 hours. Time will vary depending on oven and size of roast. To check for doneness, stick a thermometer into the thickest part of the roast. Should be 160°F. When meat is pulled out of oven, let rest for 10 minutes before slicing. Slice into portions and serve.

This is well seasoned, so no need to use a gravy

Chicken Parmesan
(Makes 4 Servings)

Ingredients:

8 oz. chicken breasts (2 Each), cut in half (4 pieces)

2 oz. Italian breadcrumbs

Egg wash (2 eggs and ¼ cup milk, beaten, mixed together)

1 cup flour

¼ stick butter

1 tsp. granulated garlic

8 oz. marinara sauce (see other recipe)

8 oz. mozzarella cheese (sliced into 1 oz. slices)

1 oz. grated Parmesan cheese

Salt and pepper to taste

Method:

Cut breasts in half, then pound out to a ½ inch thick cutlets, with a meat tenderizer. Set aside. Take 3 pans, one for seasoned flour (salt, pepper, granulated garlic), one for egg wash, and one for Italian breadcrumbs. First, heat skillet and melt butter. Add breaded cutlets and sauté. For 2 - 3 minutes each side. Set aside to cool. Place cutlets on baking sheet, top each with 2 oz. marinara sauce then top with grated parmesan cheese, and place 2 slices of mozzarella. Put into preheated oven at 350°F and bake for 7 - 10 minutes (you only want to melt cheese and bring back to temp). Serve with your favorite pasta.

The Italian section of St. Louis is called "The Hill." You can't go wrong...when in Rome...

CHAPTER 6

AH...Private Clubs!

Once I got off workers comp, I landed the general manager's position of a private club called Ocean Village. This was the club of 750 condos and a 150-seat restaurant, pool, and fitness center. The restaurant was shaped like an octagon (8 sides). Four sides faced the ocean, Everyone wanted a window table, We did tableside service including salad preparation and flaming desserts. There was an extensive wine list and a very busy early bird menu from 5:00 PM to 7:00 PM. The members were mainly composed of retired folks who wanted gourmet food for $7.95. They were angry for some reason that they were getting charged fees every month due to the restaurant losing money. My task was to get to a breakeven point, The first item on the agenda was to get rid of the early bird- worst thing to happen to Florida restaurants. Members would come in at 5:00 PM for early bird menu and stay until 10:00 PM at a window table overlooking the ocean. When the regular menu took over at 7:00 PM there were no window tables for the regular dinners. Members were tired of paying $20 to $30 for entrées instead of $7.95, Yes, they were not happy but when the extra charges on their monthly membership declined due to the restaurant breaking even the anger subsided. The second change to the restaurant was to open for lunch. Knowing that people ate with their eyes, we offered sizzling fajitas, fancy ice cream desserts in large bola glasses, and fresh seafood. One lunch I rolled up my sleeve, laid a towel on my arm and carried out a ten-pound grouper filet. Before I got back to the kitchen, I had sold the whole filet. I worked the dining room like it was my own. People ate it up...excuse the pun!

The next effort was to set up a banquet menu in house and deliver to the condos. We had a beautiful set of chafing dishes, why not do weddings in our gorgeous dining room? Why not make Hors d' Oeuvres and shrimp trees to deliver and serve in their homes at the club? Sometimes it just takes a little creativity in salesmanship. Now all of a sudden members are coming by more often, ordering foods to be delivered to their homes. Revenues increased. One evening we brought in a Dixieland band and set UP buffet tables for foods from 8 countries, kind of a grazing while they listened to the band and danced The hate turned into love

A couple weddings into our new catering venue, a man and woman came in to set up their wedding and reception. My assistant and I thought this a strange couple. They ordered a black wedding the bride was going to wear a black wedding dress. We collected a 50% deposit which was usual. They were going to have the wedding at 11:00 AM in the restaurant. They coordinated the band, flowers, and cake. On the day of the wedding the father of the bride was handing out his business card which said, "I am the father of the bride no one remembers the father, but you will remember me." We thought it was rather strange, but who are we to say what is right? When the wedding began the bride and the father walked down the aisle. When they arrived by the groom and minister, the bride's father handed off the bride's hand to the groom, collapsed and died. We called 911. My bar manager begin CPR. My bar manager did get a heartbeat, then the medics arrived. They stabilized the father and carried him out on the stretcher. A couple hours later I got a call from the groom telling me he wanted a refund. I told him we could talk in a couple days, just focus on your family's well-being. What the group didn't say is that they got married at the hospital then pulled the plug on their father's life support. My staff was in shock. To make it worse they had to clean up from the wedding from hell then get ready for dinner service. If it weren't for the fact that we were in season and was sold out with reservations, I should have called the president of the club to close for the evening. Two days later Monday, the groom called again and demanded a refund. I informed the groom that I could not refund the deposit. We ordered the food prepared and scheduled the staff. He then threatened my safety, immediately after hanging up from this nut I called my friend at the Sheriff's Department. They sent a couple of deputies to the groom's home and suggested he leave us alone. In the meantime, I had discussions with my club officials. They supported my decision.

Mushroom Strudel
(Serves 4)

Ingredients:

Meatloaf pan

1 lb. Each assortment of mushrooms (button, portabella, shitake)

2 tbsp. butter

1 oz. white wine

Salt and pepper to taste

1 oz. lemon juice

Unbaked pie shell dough (4 Each)

Method:

Preheat oven to 350° F, Melt butter in sauté pan, then add clean sliced mushrooms. Add wine, lemon juice, salt, and pepper. When it is cooked down, drain 90% of the liquid off and let cool.

Dough: Lay dough flat on work area. Place cooled mushrooms evenly on dough. Roll up into log (evenly). Place in baking pan. Brush egg wash over top/sides. Bake in a pre-heated oven until side is golden brown (15-20 minutes). Cool and serve.

A great side for a beef dish!

Pan Fried Pork Chops
(Serves 4)

Ingredients:

4 pork chops

2 oz. of Italian seasoned breadcrumbs

2 oz. margarine

2 oz. extra virgin olive oil

½ teaspoon minced garlic

Salt & pepper to taste

Method:

In a frying pan, heat oil and margarine. While that is heating place breadcrumbs in a dish and add pork chops. Cover the pork with the breadcrumbs, then place in the heated pan. Add the garlic and turn the heat down to medium. Salt & pepper as it cooks. Fry on both sides until golden brown on both sides, 4 to 5 minutes on each side. Then serve.

Easy and simple. Goes well with oven brown sweet potatoes.

Fresh Tartar Sauce
(Makes about 2 cups)

Ingredients:

½ cup Mayo

½ cup sour cream

4 oz. dill relish

1 tbsp. Lea & Perrins

Whole lemons, Juiced (2 Each)

1 tbsp. dried dill weed

Handful chopped parsley

Method:

Mix all ingredients in a bowl and chill for an hour. Serve with extra lemon wedge on plate,

Maryland Crab Cakes w/Homemade Tartar Sauce
(Makes 6 - 8 cakes)

Ingredients:

2 lb. Lump crabmeat

6-8 oz. seasoned breadcrumbs

3 oz. sweet onion finely chopped

4 oz. finely chopped celery

2 eggs

Whole lemons (2 Each)

1 clove garlic

1 small bottle of clam juice (4 oz.)

2 tbsp. Lea & Perrins Worcestershire sauce

Salt & Pepper to taste

2 oz. butter

Method:

Place crab meat gently into a mixing bowl, do not break pieces, leave whole. In a heated sauté pan melt the butter, then sauté the garlic, celery, and onions. Add to mixing bowl. Then mix in another bowl all the wet ingredients, lemon juice, clam juice, Worcestershire sauce, eggs thoroughly. Add to main ingredients and mix well. When done, you may decide to sauté or bake in oven. To sauté, melt more butter in pan and cook on each side, until golden brown.

This is just downright good eating!

CHAPTER 7

Experience The Caribbean

In an effort to expand my horizons, I checked into Holiday Inns International to see if there were any opportunities outside of the USA. I found a Holiday Inn full-service hotel in Port of Spain, Trinidad, that was looking for a general manager. I met with the owner in Miami to discuss the opening. We liked what each other had to say and he offered me the position. I went back to my condo on Vero Beach and told my roommate who was a golf pro at the local Golf Club. He found a roommate to take my place and off I went to Trinidad. My roommate drove me to Palm Beach International Airport where I flew out to the last group of islands in the Caribbean before you get to the Atlantic Ocean. The trip was only 1,200 miles but it seemed like we stopped at every island on the route. It took the better part of the day and evening. The plane finally touchdown just before midnight,

This was my first experience of going through immigration, but I had my brand-new passport, and an international driver's license, as well as papers galore. I'm called up to the immigration officer at the desk, hand him my papers and stand back. His first question, "Are you here for leisure or work?" To which I quickly responded, "To work here." I began to tell him that I was the new general manager of the Holiday Inn, Port of Spain. He then cut me off and asked where my work papers were. "My work papers?" I'm thinking under my breath. "I don't have any stinking work papers." Instead, I just said that I was not told about working papers. The officer said without papers I could not enter the country. It's about 12:30 AM by now, which meant no more flights back to the US. Without hesitation he raised his hand and two guards armed with Thompson Submachine guns approached his desk. I was escorted to a jail cell at the airport. I asked the officer if I could call the hotel to let the owner, who was waiting for me, know that I was being held in a cell at the airport. The officer again quickly responded within emphatic "No." Now I'm in the cell and a BIWI representative (that's the airlines name) walked by me. I asked if he would call the hotel to let the owner know where I am. About an hour passed and the immigration officer appeared at my cell. I could see he was irritated. He orders the guard to release me, but not before he looks me in the eye and said to me, "This is not over." I got into a cab and asked the driver to take me to the hotel.

It had just begun to rain, and the taxi driver had his head out the window driving down the road. I asked him why he wasn't using the wiper blades to which he responded, "There's no rubber on the blades, and it would scratch the windshield." In a strange evening as this I almost didn't give it another thought. I'd find out later that this was just one part of living on an island. Trinidad used to be a colony of the British Empire and gained its independence back in the 1960s. Without British financial assistance Trinidad had become a third world country so to speak. You'd see people on bicycles with no tires, no new cars, people walking or taking the bus to get places.

Back to the story. When I reached the hotel, I was impressed with its size...17 stories. There was a 14 ft. wall around the perimeter of property, which I thought was odd. Holiday Inn doesn't usually require some type of property line acknowledgement. Fourteen feet to me was overkill. The owner was in the lobby to greet me. He apologized for the ordeal at the airport. He said it was his mistake. He neglected to tell me that I should have said I was in Trinidad for pleasure not work. I was escorted to my suite where I would live while I was in the county. It was quite a nice living room, dining room, kitchen, bedroom, and a huge balcony.

I had just fallen asleep when the phone rang at about 3:00 AM. It was the immigration officer from the airport. He reiterated his last words to me upon being released along with an "I'll get you for this." I found out later that the hotel owner had called the president of Trinidad, who in turn called the head of immigration and ordered him to let me out. So, it would be safe to say that immigration was ticked off. Three days later, the owner came to me and let me know I had been deported. He asked me if I'd like to go back to the states until he could fix this mess. He had another hotel on the beach in the island country of Granada. I chose Granada. I was driven back to the airport and caught a puddle jumper plane (about 12 seats) to Granada. This time when I arrived at immigration, I told the officer I was on vacation I really was on vacation. There were no doors in the hotel lobby. I got out of the taxi and entered the hotel through the front. All I saw was beach and ocean. I walked up to the front desk and was greeted upon my arrival to the Ramada Renaissance Resort. It was beautiful! Even the picture on the wall of President Reagan shaking hands with the owner was beautiful. For you history buffs, when President Reagan was in office the United States, he invaded Granada due to the fact that Cuba had invaded Granada. In the process, the Americans had blown up the old Ramada. Thanks to the taxpayers of the USA, the Corps of Engineers built a new hotel bigger and better. I was proud to be an American! Granada wasn't quite as poor as Trinidad, but also wasn't much better. For the next 10 days I relaxed on the beach, ate, and drank to my content. It was a sad day when I received a phone call telling me my papers were now in order and I hopped on the puddle jumper back to Port of Spain.

My first day back in Trinidad, I got the grand tour of the capital city of Port of Spain. It was very dirty, and the citizens were very poor. I'm thinking, "How could the hotel stay in business if conditions were this bad?" I was instructed by the owner to bring along a doorman to accompany me when I left the hotel. These guys looked like they were the frontline of the Green Bay Packers. They were huge. I had a vehicle at my disposal. I was paid in TT dollars, which were approximately ¼th of the value compared to our U.S. dollars. I say this because the owner charged hotel guests in US dollars and paid the employees in TT dollars-very shrewd. The hotel employees were extremely friendly, and the women were quite beautiful. The citizens were a mix of Chinese, Indian, African, and Spanish. They were much friendlier than my experience at the airport. (TT dollars were short for Trinidad/Tobago dollars.)

Almost all of the clientele were from outside of the country, especially the U.S. The guests had no problem with the room rates. We had 4 large banquet rooms, able to hold 300 or 400 people. The majority of business was weddings, anniversary parties, business meetings during the week, and etc. On the 17th floor, there was a second restaurant besides the main dining room off the lobby. This was a revolving restaurant. Once every hour the restaurant revolved. The first evening I worked on the 17th floor I was talking to some guests. What I didn't know was that the kitchen did not revolve as the restaurant did. I went into the kitchen to ask the chef a question posed by the guest. When I received the answer, I proceeded back to the dining room, only to find that I had lost my table. It took a minute to gather my bearings and find my guests.

After a few weeks, I was lonely for some female companionship. I asked a young lady out from our accounting department. She was a tall, slender lady with a gorgeous smile. She said, "OK." I drove over to her home and knocked on the door to be greeted by her mother. My date was 28 years old, but the culture in Trinidad was that you lived at home until you were married. So, I had the good fortune of meeting the parents. We chatted for a while. Finally, I looked at my watch and said we had a reservation at a restaurant. We said our goodbyes and begun to head toward the door. Her sister followed close by. I asked my date what was going on and she told me that her sister was our chaperone for the evening. Wonderful! It was a bit of a shock, but when in Rome, do as the Romans. Apparently, I was trusted a little more because we had no chaperone on the second date. Foreign cultures can be strange. The next weekend, I drove myself to the beach. I found almost all of my employees including my date with their families. The woman were all topless! Not that I'm complaining, but that's the difference in cultures from one country to another. So I took off my top.

Being on an island took some getting used to the shortages. One day at the grocery store, I went to the dairy case for some cheese. The entire cheese case was filled with cheddar cheese. I asked a clerk if there were any other types of cheese, to which he replied, "Not until the next cargo ship arrived." The meat case was the same. You were a captive of what was on the next ship.

Shortly after, I spent some time on the main kitchen of the hotel. The chef was a very pleasant man who cared greatly for the whole hotel staff. He had been employed for about 15 years. Everyone knew and loved him. One day, I noticed it took a long time to get some food out of the kitchen. I asked the chef to tell me what the issue was. He told me that most of the equipment was broken or had missing parts. The maintenance guys had robbed one piece of equipment to repair another. It had gotten to the point where there was no more equipment to take from to do repairs. I called an equipment repair company and ask them to do an estimate of repairing all the equipment. He came up with a bit of over $200,000 in US dollars. He then told me it would take 6 months to a year to get the parts - that's living on an island. I gave the estimate to the owner with all the part parts. He looked at it and then tossed it into the trash. He stated that the kitchen didn't need any parts and walked away. Apparently, one of my predecessors had attempted to obtain parts as well. At this point, the owner was only concerned about pulling all the revenue out of the hotel, as he was able. I never did see a financial report. Ever!

One morning, I came down the elevator to the lobby to grab a bite of breakfast. When I arrived in the lobby there were 6- or 7-men wearing FBI windbreakers. I walked up to one gentleman, introduced myself and asked him what was going on. After he asked some pointed questions as to who I was, he told me that the FBI suspected the owner of smuggling drugs from South America through Trinidad to Miami. The FBI agent strongly suggested that I check in at the USA embassy to be on the safe side. The next morning, I drove down to the embassy. However, silly me, I thought that our embassies were guarded by US Marines. Well, I was wrong. The local militia guarded our embassy in Trinidad. The line of people looking to immigrate from Trinidad to the USA wrapped around the block and passed the next block. I found a side door, entered, and attempted to find an American citizen. That didn't happen, but at least they knew I was in the country. In the meantime, Florida was about to get hit with hurricane Andrew. I called my tenants. They had all been ordered to move inland and out of the way. Fortunately for them, and my condo, the hurricane hit Florida just below Miami. Homestead was wiped off the map with category 5 winds. There was only one flight open in Miami, so it took 3 days to catch a flight out of Trinidad to the US to see what damages my condo actually sustained. Finally, on the 3rd day, I arrived at the airport at 2 AM. I stood in line for 2 hours and boarded the only plane going to the states. Once I arrived in Miami, I decided to stay in the states for the next 6 to 8 months, and I lived off the money that I had saved in Trinidad.

Roasted Poblano Banana Butter
(Makes 3 Cups)

Ingredients:

2 large ripe bananas

1 cup heavy cream

1 cup butter, softened

2 roasted poblano, diced small

Method:

Mash bananas thoroughly to a puree. Reduce banana puree with heavy cream by half. Then, whisk in butter on low heat until mixture has solidified, before serving. Remove from heat, and fold in poblano peppers. Serve over any fresh grilled fish.

This is excellent over any grilled seafood.

Guacamole
(Makes 2 Cups)

Ingredients:

3 large ripe avocados (prefer Haas)

1 - 2 tbsp. lime juice

4 – 5 drops of Frank's hot sauce

1 med. diced plum tomatoes

1 tsp. ground cumin

Salt and pepper to taste

Dash granulated garlic

1 tbsp. Lea & Perrins

1 tsp. dried oregano

Method:

Remove avocado from outer skin and remove seed from center. Place in mixing bowl. Thoroughly mash up avocado pulp. Add rest of ingredients a little at a time and mix. Serve with tortilla chips or as side with fajitas.

Guacamole makes all dishes better!

Picante Sauce (For Fajitas)
(Makes 1 Cup)

Ingredients:

½ cucumber peeled & diced ½" cubes

Plum tomatoes cut to same size as cucumbers (3 Each)

½ red onions cut same as above

½ oz. extra virgin olive oil

Salt and pepper to taste

½ oz. balsamic vinegar

½ tsp. granulated garlic

½ tsp. dried oregano

½ tsp. dried basil

Lime juice (Squeezed) (1 Each)

Method:

Cut all veggies into ½" cubes, then add rest of ingredients. Toss thoroughly. Serve.

The Balsamic vinegar adds a flavor I've never tasted in a picante.

Spanish Rice
(Serves 4 - 6)

Ingredients:

½ lb. Mahatma Rice, long grain

7-8 oz can diced tomatoes (Plain) (1 Each)

½ red onion finely chopped

1 tsp. cumin

Salt and pepper to taste

1-2 tbsp. Lea & Perrins

Salt and pepper to taste

1 tsp. granulated garlic

1 tsp. Mexican Oregano (If you can't find, use regular oregano.)

2 qt. water

2 tbsp. extra virgin olive oil

Method:

In a 3 qt. sauce pot, bring water to boil. Add 1 tsp. sea salt, then add rice. Cook until al dente, (cooked, but still firm). Rinse off in colander with cold water to stop cooking. Set aside to drain. In a skillet, heat olive oil and add chopped onions. When translucent, then add rice and diced tomatoes. Mix thoroughly, then add seasoning. Taste and adjust seasoning if necessary. Rice will finish cooking during the process by soaking up spices and juices.

This is good stuff! You can use this as a side dish or in a burrito or fajita.

Paella
(Mexican Casserole, Serves 8)

Ingredients:

1 lb. Mahatma long grain rice

1 lb. hot Italian sausage, sliced into ½" rounds

1 lb. boneless/skinless chicken thigh (diced ½" cubes) (I prefer boneless/skinless

thighs)

1 lb. 31 – 35 shrimp, peeled and deveined including tails

1 ½ lb. black Belgium mussels

1 pinch saffron, or 1 tsp. ground turmeric

3 tbsp. Lea & Perrins

Salt and pepper to taste

1 tsp. ground garlic

1 tbsp. Mexican oregano

½ red onion finely chopped

¼ cup extra virgin olive oil

1 tsp. dried basil

3 qt. water

8 oz. cans diced tomatoes & green chilies (2 Each)

Method:

In a large sauce pot, add water and bring to boil. Add a little salt, then pour in rice and stir. Cook rice until al dente. Wash off in colander with cold water, then drain. Set aside. In a large skillet, heat with olive oil then add sausage that you cut into ½" rounds. Brown sausage then add chicken and do same. Add onion, sauté until onion is translucent. Add tomatoes. Then shrimp and mussels (right at end). When mussels have opened, they are done. If they do not open, discard. Add rest of ingredients and lightly but thoroughly mix. Note: The authentic pan to make paella is a large flat skillet about 3' around, but most people do not have this equipment.

Just like Mamacita used to make.

Hawaiian Marinade
(For Grilling Steaks)

Ingredients:

46 oz. can pineapple juice (1 Each)

1 cup soy sauce

½ cup brown sugar

1 tbsp. granulated garlic

1 tbsp. ground ginger

Method:

Mix all ingredients in a bowl. Marinate steaks for 12 – 24 hours before grilling.

This is great if you're grilling steaks, especially ribeye steaks.

Conch Fritters
(Serves Party Of 15 - 20)

Ingredients:

3 green peppers, minced

3 red peppers, minced

3 jalapenos, minced

3 red onions, minced

1 qt. heavy cream

8 eggs

5 lbs. conch meat

3 tbsp. baking powder

2 tbsp. black pepper

2 tbsp. salt

1 tbsp. Old Bay Seasoning

2 cups flour

3 tbsp. fresh cilantro finely chopped

½ cup Franks Hot sauce

Method:

Combine all ingredients in large bowl, except flour. Wearing rubber gloves, fold in flour until it is completely incorporated. Portion with 1 oz. and deep fry for 2 – 3 minutes. Serve with remoulade sauce.

Herb Crusted Florida Grouper
(Serves 2)

Ingredients:

8 oz. Grouper filet, seasoned with breadcrumbs (2 Each)

1 oz. butter

1 oz. olive oil

Lemon, juiced (1 Each)

1 oz. white wine

Salt and pepper to taste

2 oz. sundried tomato relish

Method:

Dredge grouper in breadcrumbs. Melt butter and oil in saucepan and place grouper into pan, season with salt and pepper. Brown on both sides. Deglaze with lemon juice and wine. Top with sundried tomato relish.

Grouper is a slightly stronger fish. The tomato relish will compliment very well.

Sundried Tomato Relish
(Serves 4 - 6)

Ingredients:

1 cup sundried tomatoes

½ cup roasted corn

2 roasted poblano peppers

1 bunch fresh basil

½ cup olive oil

1 tsp. fresh garlic

Method:

Julienne sundried tomatoes, basil and poblano peppers. Toss in large bowl with corn, olive oil and garlic. Add salt and pepper to taste.

Macadamia Nut & Banana Chip Encrusted Local Yellowtail Snapper

Ingredients:

8 oz. Yellowtail snapper filet (1 filet per person)

2 oz. Macadamia nuts (crushed)

3 oz. all-purpose flour

2 oz. dried banana chips

1 oz. Olive oil

3 oz. Butter

3 oz. Caramelized plantains (sliced)

Method:

Dredge snapper in flour, then egg wash, and place face down into macadamia nut/banana mixture. Sauté in olive oil to a light golden brown, finish in oven 350° F. 4 - 5 minutes.

Cream Sauce For Yellowtail Snapper

Ingredients:

1 cup heavy cream

½ cup Frangelico liquor

Method:

In a saucepan, heat and reduce cream, (do not boil). When reduced by half, add the Frangelico. Serve over snapper.

Macadamia nuts are substituted for breadcrumbs. Big flavor improvement

Caribbean Citrus Relish
(Makes 18 Servings)

Ingredients:

½ Pineapple

½ Cantaloupe

½ Honey Dew

Kiwi (2 Each)

Mango (1 Each)

Green onions (3 Each)

½ tbsp. Jerk spice

Method:

Dice all fruit. Mix together in a bowl. Then add Jerk spice.

Dice all ingredients finely. It can be used by spooning over top of grilled fish or pork or chicken.

Fresh Pan Seared Sea Scallops
(Serves 4)

Ingredients:

8 oz. sea scallops (make sure membrane is removed)

1 oz. Dusting of Cajun spices

1 oz. extra virgin olive oil

Method:

Heat saucepan and oil. Put scallops that have been rubbed in Cajun seasoning into pan. Cook on each side for 2 – 3 minutes. Do not overcook.

This is a decadent way to make sea scallops.

Adobo Sauce
(Yields 1 Quart)

Ingredients:

3 oz. sliced onion

2 cloves garlic

Canola oil

10 guajillo chilis, seeded

½ tsp. cumin

½ tsp. whole white pepper

1 cinnamon stick

1 cup water

½ cup honey

¼ cup sherry wine vinegar

Salt and pepper to taste

Method:

Sauté onions and garlic in hot oil until onions are translucent. Add chilies, cumin, pepper, and cinnamon. Fry chilies until they turn a dark brick red color. Add enough water to cover in blender. Boil until chilies are soft. Drain, reserving water. In a blender, mix chili mixture with reserved water until a paste-like consistency is achieved. Add honey, vinegar, and salt until a balance of flavor is achieved.

This is a sauce that can stand up to chicken or pork dishes.

Steak Fajitas
(Makes 8 - 10 Fajitas)

Ingredients:

1 large package of flour tortilla shells

2 lb. Flank steak sliced thin (¼" thick strips)

1 large green pepper

1 large red or yellow pepper

1 med. red onion

2 oz. Lea & Perrins

2 oz. red wine

1 oz. soy sauce

5 oz. water

1 tbsp. granulated garlic

1 tbsp. cracked black pepper

1 tbsp. dried basil

1 tsp. dried oregano

8 oz. cup sour cream (1 Each)

1 cup picante sauce (See recipe on other page)

1 cup guacamole (See recipe on other page)

1 tsp. ground cumin

Lime (1 Each)

Method:

First slice Flank into ½" strips (always cut against grain). Place into large mixing bowl, and add water, soy sauce, wine, Lea & Perrins, garlic, basil, and pepper. Let marinade for at least 1 hour (overnight is best). Cut peppers and onions into long strips. Then take meat out of marinate, place into preheated large skillet, to begin sautéing. Add peppers and onions as well. When veggies are fork tender, add oregano, cumin, salt & pepper to taste (taste before adding salt). Serve with warm tortilla shells (**DO NOT MICROWAVE**). Add picante, guacamole, and sour cream on the side.

The flank steak is tender and flavorful.

CHAPTER 8

What To Do Now?

Now a free man, my thoughts began to wander. I called my ex-wife Sholeh and was invited up to Kansas City. She moved back with the family after our divorce. I settled in for a few days, when I received a call about a FBD position open just off Hilton Head Island. It was a private club on Daufuskee Island called the Melrose club. Daufuskee Island was famous due to the fact that John F. Kennedy, Jr. honeymooned on the island. I was offered the position and accepted. Out of convenience, the president of the club let me stay in one of the cottages until I could find a place to live. It was a large operation. Even though my position was on the 3rd tier of the management pyramid, I managed just under 100 staff. There was a Jack Nicklaus golf course on the club, as well as a grocery store owned by the club. It was a neat situation. If you were on the 9th tee you could pick up the phone, call in your lunch order, and drive UP to the window at the store. Just like McDonalds, except this was good food, then drive your golf cart to the 10th tee without losing your spot on the course.

The store was a great amenity for the club. When you made reservations to stay at the club you could order your groceries from the grocery store. It was delivered to the cottage before the member arrived. We added some pre-made from scratch as well as the usual things like milk and eggs, etc. There were 5 food and beverage outlets. The fine dining room was over the main lobby at the end. It was open Friday nights through Sunday brunch. We had an excellent array of wines and of course the lobsters, filets of beef, and specialty wild game. On Friday and Saturday evenings, I would maître'd the wines. On special occasions, we would do buffets like Easter and Mother's Day. We received all our supplies through barges, so shopping for ice blocks for carvings was impossible. Instead, we would carve figures out of tallow, which were purified blocks of lard. The buffets were gorgeous. The members were from 48 states and 9 countries, and they would take photos of our outrageous buffets.

Our catering department booked wedding receptions of some of the CEOs of the largest companies in the country. One wedding reception cost a quarter million dollars. Our Catering Director made $25,000 from that single event. On another occasion, we booked a wedding and reception for this member. It was scheduled for March 10th, which is usually mild at Hilton head, at this time of year, but a super storm was brewing in the Gulf of Mexico. By the time it reached South Carolina it was pushing 80 mile per hour winds. The wedding was to take place outside the mansion. The morning of the storm, my executive chef, my roommate and the fine dining restaurant manager and I were the only people to make it over on the boat. Next, the power goes off, the band did not make it over, and neither did the wedding cake. We had a trio that played at the pre-wedding dinner the night before the wedding. By the way, all of the rooms and cottages were full of wedding guests that came in the week before so they could enjoy playing golf and nature. We talked to the bride's parents and suggested preparing some cold Hors d' Oeuvres. Of course, the parents were freaking out. The father of the bride was feeding his wife pills and scotch to calm her down. The brother wanted to play a round of golf, thinking he could hit the ball 300 yards backed with 80 mile per hour winds. To say the least, it was a mess. We wrapped our heads around the situation. Chef said that if we could get the gas grills up and running, we could put out this extravagant seafood buffet. We got the trio to play for the reception. Our bakery made some cakes. So at least the party would have cake for the ceremony. Believe it or not, we pulled it off. We had the entire seafood buffet set in our gourmet dining room. They had their dance floor and beautifully decorated tables with our finest. We received a standing ovation from everyone at the wedding. For weeks afterwards, we heard from members all over the country expressing congratulations. A few weeks after all the goodwill, a new company was contracted to run the day-to-day operations. We were all out of our jobs.

Roasted Corn/Avocado Salad
(Serves 6)

Ingredients:

First Part:

6 fresh ears of corn, shucked

Extra virgin olive oil (Just enough to rub on ears of corn)

Salt and pepper to taste

Second Part:

Ripe avocados, diced in ½" cubes (2 Each)

1 large cucumber, peeled & diced into ½" cubes

1/6 red onion chopped finely

1 either red or yellow pepper chopped into ½" pieces

½ cup lemon juice

1/8 cup extra virgin olive oil

Salt and pepper to taste

Method:

1st Part: Take fresh shucked corn, rub olive oil covering ears with your hands. Then sprinkle salt and pepper over each ear. Either roast in oven in baking dish, or char-broil on outside grill. Let cool, then cut corn off cob.
2nd Part: In a mixing bowl, add corn, avocados, cucumber, pepper, onion, lemon juice, olive oil and mix thoroughly.

Taste then season with salt & pepper. Taste best if served at room temperature.

A light summer salad best served when you are able to get fresh sweet corn.

Pumpkin Soup
(Serves 10 – 12)

Ingredients:

1 large pumpkin, cored out (optional)

2 large cans of pumpkin about 44 oz. - 48 oz.

1 qt. heavy cream

2 tsp. Ground Cinnamon

1 tsp. Ground nutmeg

½ tsp. vanilla

6 oz. brown sugar

Method:

(Optional: Carve out large pumpkin and set aside). Add pumpkin, cream to large saucepan, and slowly heat, as not to curdle cream. When hot, add spices and brown sugar. Mix thoroughly, (if you are looking for the "wow" factor, heat whole pumpkin in 300° F oven until inside is hot. Pour hot soup into pumpkin, and place on buffet/dining room table. Heated Pumpkin will keep soup hot for 30 – 45 minutes.)

*Note: Soup should be as thick as a chowder

This will be the centerpiece of your Holiday table.

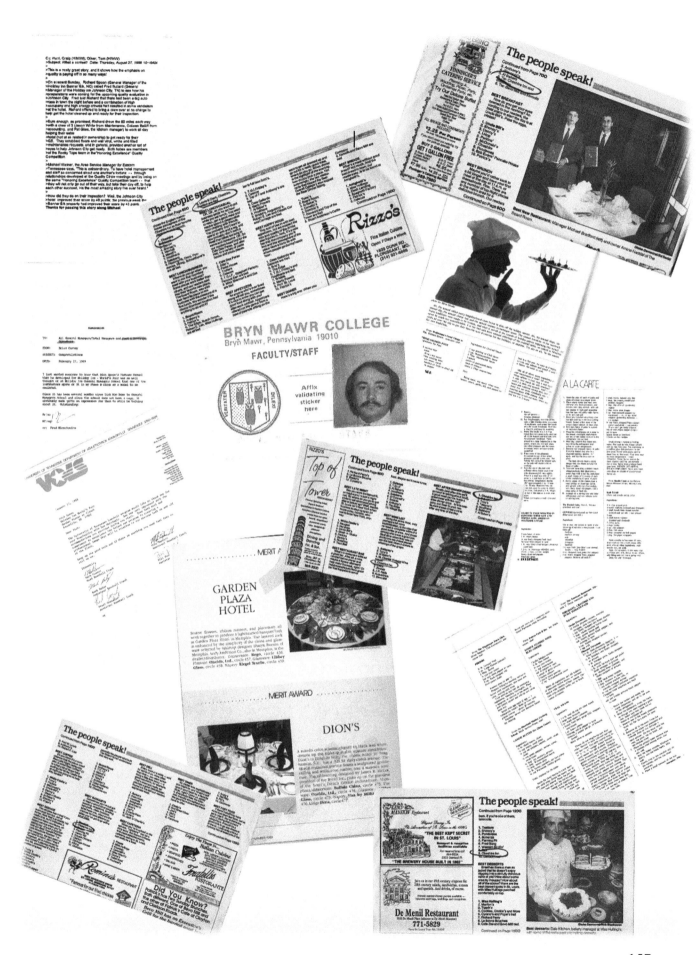

BRYN MAWR COLLEGE
Bryn Mawr, Pennsylvania 19010

FACULTY/STAFF

Affix
validating
sticker
here

CHAPTER 9

Life In The Mountains Of North Carolina

About that time, I called my old friend and mentor, Mr. Gibson. He was now an area manager for Cooper Hotels. He had a small but important full-service Holiday Inn in Banner Elk, North Carolina. It was a nice little hotel of 101 guest rooms, a restaurant and banquet facilities. The prior manager wasn't spending much time at the hotel due to illness in his immediate family. The hotel had failed two Holiday Inn inspections in a row and out of 2,540 full-service hotels in the US, it was ranked 2,420. They were about to lose their franchise. This was as bad as it gets in the industry. The hotel was dirty, the employees were not friendly to the guests, and most importantly there were life and safety violations. My job was to hit the ground running and solve the safety issues. The first issue was the fire system over the gas cooking equipment in the kitchen. Apparently, according to the Holiday Inn standards, this system was obsolete, and the screens were dripping with grease. Fortunately, my catering person's father was the Fire Marshall. So, I called him to have him inspect the hoods fire system. He came to the hotel, we met, had coffee, and then walked into the kitchen. He looked at the system and told me it was fine and totally within code, even though there were more modern systems on the market. I asked him if he would sign off on what he told me, and he said he would if I would call a hood cleaning company to steam clean all the grease from the hood. He provided me with a company's phone number, and I called. One week later, we had a clean hood and certification for the system. $300 later, the Holiday Inn Corporation took us off the failing notice with life/safety issues.

The next item on the agenda was to find a fix for the brand-new fireplace in the lobby that was spewing out soot when it was in use. I called the original contractor to stop the flow of soot to our guests' lungs and eyes. He gave me an estimate of $10 to reroute the chimney and a lot of double talk. Somehow, I just didn't believe him. Then I called the gas company. To get them out quickly, I told him I smelled gas. Propane doesn't have an odor, but the gas company puts in additive to their gas so if there is a leak, you will smell it. They rushed out to the hotel. The tech person looked at the fireplace immediately said there is your problem. I asked him what was the problem? He told me he had he told me we had unvented logs we needed vented logs. I asked how much the vented logs were, and he told me about $350 dollars. Are you serious? I asked him to get the proper logs out to the hotel ASAP. A week later we had a perfectly running fireplace. We also had to replace all the acoustical ceiling tiles because they were smudged with soot.

My predecessor told the Engineering Department to use white oil-based paint to cover up the tiles. What a cluster. On the next visit from the owner and his family he saw the fireplace working. He called me out to the lobby. In an agitated tone of voice, he said, "I thought I told you not to turn the fireplace on due to the issues?" I asked him if he saw any soot in the air. He looked around and said, "No." I like to play mind games sometimes. Rather than outright telling him it was no longer an issue, I toyed with him for a while, then I told him it was a simple fix. He was so happy to see his expensive mountain retreat fireplace working perfectly. He and his family enjoyed their stay after he calm down. We had dinner that evening off property. I let him know there would be some big changes in the coming months.

My first big challenge was to bring our team members up to par with plenty of training and a large attitude adjustment. I called the entire team together for an employee meeting. I was brutally honest and told them that the hotel was losing money and we were in the bottom 100 ranking out of some 2,500 full-service Holiday Inns across the nation. The hotel had just gone through a $1,000,000 renovation and it looked old and tired. The first question I asked that team was, "In your opinion, what can we do to get the scores up?" I wasn't just looking at getting out of the basement with our ratings I wanted us to be winners! They came up with some great ideas. I wrote the ideas on the chalk board then printed out a copy for all. We got back to the basics. Each department had a cork board with three lists, "do, doing, and done." Management 101. We had daily meetings with each department to go over our list of to-do's and moved the tasks across the boards to completed. On their lists we had general cleaning repairs, touch up paint, etc. Winning awards was a bit stressful. One team member told me reaching for number one was hard. I asked him, "If it were easy then wouldn't everyone be winning?" He thought about it for a minute then agreed.

The next item was to communicate our progress. We did this in our daily, weekly, and monthly meetings. Every new team member hired went through a three-day orientation. This not only included training, but a history of the area landmarks and directions. Part of the training included the greeting. When a guest came through the front doors they were immediately welcomed as they entered. Anytime a guest asked a question, my team would respond with the correct answer. When the guest thanked the team member, the member would respond with, "It's my pleasure." If there was a situation where the team member could not answer the guest, they would find someone that could properly help our guest. To tell a guest, "I don't know" was simply unacceptable.

With all this training, the members needed some type of motivation to keep moving in an upward direction. To accomplish this, we came up with some small tokens of appreciation. For example, when our front desk would obtain a score of 90% or better, each member would receive a $10 cash bonus for each month that they hit their score. Housekeeping ran a similar contest for guest rooms and bath cleanliness. Each member of housekeeping would get $10. This was a low-income area for our team, so $10 was a welcome benefit. Well, the hotel began to look and smell cleaner. With the scores going up, employees smiled more. It was nice to hear the guests that were checking out compliment the hotel staff on how clean and fresh the hotel looked. By the end of our first year, the hotel had moved up to 715th place from 2420. In celebration, we had a big dinner for all our team and their spouses. We began an employee of the month program. The prize was $50 cash, their name on a large plaque in the lobby, and their own personal plaque. Turnover among the staff dropped from 300% per year to 25%. People received promotions to manager and supervisor positions. We developed menus, photographed the plate presentation, and wrote recipes. All of a sudden, we had consistency. This brought townspeople back for lunch and dinner. We began a Sunday brunch. On Father's and Mother's Day, fathers and mothers ate for free when they brought their families into the restaurant. Then we began a Friday night fish fry and a Saturday night prime rib buffet. Revenues went up. All of a sudden, the food department made a profit! That allowed the hotel to run a profit to turn a profit now that the food was covering their expenses. Ownership was happy! There is more to running a hotel than good service and a good product. Our community standing had taken a big hit from prior management. The locals had a bad taste in their mouth, excuse the pun, from the bad food, poor service, and dirty guestrooms. Townspeople used to send their visiting guests to our hotel, until it got so bad that they swore off the property. So, I joined Rotary and made sales calls to invite locals back from for a second chance. They liked what they saw! We decided to adopt the local elementary school up the road. To begin we had lunch with Santa Claus, which was a successful idea from the past. This created a positive stir with locals. Many had children at the school. We took photos of 150 children from 1st through 3rd grades individually sitting on Santa's lap. Of course, we fed them lunch with the help of our grocery vendor. It was nothing fancy, just chicken tenders and fries, but these were simple folks.

Then, we tried something new. The principle, guidance counselor, and I, all picked a family going through hard times. We obtained the children's first name, age, and clothing sizes. The housekeeping ladies were in charge of donating clothing purchased new or used. The front desk and maintenance were responsible for toys. We asked the parents what each child's toy wish was, and the food department and

I would gather the items. I managed to negotiate with our food vendor to get bulk items at cost. I asked my Rotary brothers and sisters for cash donations. They came through big time! On the first year of this project, my managers and I were discussing the progress we were making in the lobby. A guest checking in overheard us talking about the family. He heard that the oldest son sold his computer to help the family pay doctor's bills for the father. He was touched. He asked what were we going to do? I spoke up that a new or used computer was a little out of our price range. He spoke up and said, "Don't worry. I will donate a new computer for the son." God surely works in mysterious ways! The day we were delivering all the gifts to the family we made sure it was the day the kids were in school. We drove up to the house and the mother immediately burst into tears. Then of course all of my team and I did the same It really affected my team. They understood at that point there was always someone worse off than yourself. The whole attitude of the hotel employees changed for the good after that day. A year later we were getting closer to our goal of winning the top award. We broke the top 100 in our guest service scores. We were due for our next inspection. Just a reminder, when I first arrived at the hotel two years prior, we had scored a 715 on our inspection, out of a possible 1,000. Passing was a 750 score. My team busted their backsides getting ready. We scored a 960 out of 1,000...Fantastic for a 27-year-old hotel! Our Holiday Inn inspector told us he had never seen such a transformation in a hotel. That score put us over the top and we won our "Torchbearer award." We were in the top 5% of the nation for quality of product in our service.

Another community project we were thrown into was at the beginning of winter in 1998. It was late November, and we received over a foot of snow. That's not normally an issue up in the mountains, but it had rained for the next 5 days, adding 10 inches of rain to the snow. The area encountered flash flooding. Several small towns in the area were literally washed away. People lost their lives and homes. My management team put our heads together to come up with ideas how to make a sizable chunk of money. Since Banner Elk, North Carolina was known as the "Fraser Fur Christmas Tree Capital Of The Country," we decided to talk with some of the tree farmers and ask for tree donations to sell in our parking lot. The farmers were glad to help we even found someone to make us a bunch of wreaths. We had a small camping trailer, which we used to keep warm in the evening and took turns. Toward the end of our tree sale, one of my Rotary brothers went live remotely from the local radio station. People flocked into the parking lot and purchased every last tree and wreath. We were able to donate over $2000 to the local food bank.

The next winter began almost snowless. Cooper Hotels invited all the general managers on a cruise to Cozumel, Cancun, and Key West. Although I had been in Cancun several times, I had never been on a cruise. The general managers and officers of Cooper Hotels met at Fort Lauderdale to board the ship It was a great time! When the ship docked, in Cozumel, there were several options to do once on shore. I chose the boat ride to this deserted beach. The drinks were flowing, we were all getting sunburned on the small boat ride back to Cozumel, and they had a drinking contest. The rules were simple, whoever could open a bottle of beer, chug it, then turn the bottle upside down over their head without anything coming out was the winner. Well, guess who won? Yours truly! Of course, my prize was a bottle of tequila...just what a drunk person needs. When we all stepped back on land, we all decided to get some lunch to soak up some of the liquor in our stomachs. We found Carlos and Charles. After a great lunch, they formed a Congo line, so we all got in line. At one end of the line, was a bartender with a goatskin pouch pouring tequila shots down our throats. Most of us were drinking margaritas at lunch, so the idea of the food soaking the alcohol up went down the drain literally. I had to get some Cuban cigars to go home with me. I paid my portion of the check and excused myself to find a cigar store. I stumbled out the restaurant, took a right, and stumbled down the street. I got to the end of the entertainment area, turned around, and headed back the other way. Finally, I got so tired of stumbling down the street that I hailed a taxi. Upon entering the taxi, I told the driver to take me to the closest cigar store. He took me less than one city block and stopped. I inquired as to why he stopped the taxi. He pointed to the cigar store just one door to the left of Carlos and Charlies. I walked almost a mile, and the store was only 20 feet to the left. I paid the driver and went to the store. I selected about 10 luscious cigars, paid for them, and walked back to the ship docked across the street. Most of the general managers missed dinner on this ship that evening. I had no clue as to why. The next morning, I asked a couple of ship people how I could get the cigars passed the people on duty. One suggested I go down to the Purser's Office and pick up a couple large envelopes. I did. When we arrived in Key West, I exited the ship and found a mailbox on a corner. Two days later, I got the cigars in my mailbox in Banner Elk, North Carolina.

A few days later, we got hit with a 42-inch Blizzard. We lost power in the hotel. Not even the toilets worked. My front desk team had to work the front desk in their pajamas since no one could come and go...we were snowed in! Of course, we had a full house with it being a ski weekend. The guests ate a lot of cold food. No one went hungry. We did attempt to cook some sausage and biscuits, but we had to keep the back door of the kitchen open to eliminate the gas fumes. Too much work for so little benefit. Someone had a battery-operated radio. We heard that the governor had declared an emergency and the National Guard was coming up to help the area. Now our county had but one snowplow. It took three days just to plow the only main road in the county. When the National Guard arrived, we were disappointed to find only two Humvees with two guardsmen in each to assist us. We finally shoveled our way out five days later.

Portabella Fries
(Serves 3 – 4)

Ingredients:

2 lbs. portabella mushrooms, cut into strips

¼ cup all-purpose flour, sifted

3 eggs, 1 pt. milk (egg wash)

½ cup savory breading

Canola oil for frying, heated to 350° F

Ingredients for Savory Breading:

1 can of Panko Breadcrumbs

8 oz. finely grated Parmigiano-Reggiano cheese

1 oz. cracked black pepper

1 oz. crushed red pepper flakes

¼ cup finely chopped Italian parsley

¼ cup finely chopped fresh mint

¼ cup finely grated lemon peel

¼ cup finely grated orange peel

Method:

Clean and stem mushrooms. Cut into ½-inch-thick strips. Dredge mushrooms strips in flour, (seasoned with salt, pepper, garlic) then shake off excess flour. Place mushrooms strips in egg wash, then dip in savory breading. Place breaded strips in hot oil for 2 – 3 minutes, until golden brown. Drain and serve hot.

A great substitute for French fries

Sanibel Crusted Shrimp & Scallop Scampi
(Makes 2 Servings)

Ingredients:

6 Large shrimp, peeled and deveined

4 oz. bay scallops

¼ tsp. granulated garlic

1 lemon, juiced

1 tsp. sweet basil

2 oz. seasoned breadcrumbs

Salt and pepper to taste

1 oz. olive oil

1 oz. butter

1 oz. white wine

Method:

Dredge shrimp and scallops in breadcrumbs. In heated sauté pan, melt butter & oil. When hot, drop in shrimp and scallops, then add garlic and basil. Add lemon juice and wine last minute and simmer. Season with salt and pepper.

The breadcrumbs add a whole new texture to the scampi

Banyan's Coconut Shrimp
(Makes 21 To 26 Pieces)

Ingredients:

21 - 26 shrimp peeled and deveined

4 oz. all-purpose flour

½ tsp. baking powder

1 bottle of beer

¼ oz. coconut (shredded)

Salt and pepper to taste

Method:

In a medium mixing bowl, add flour, coconut, salt, and pepper. Whip in the beer until batter will stick to whip. Dredge shrimp in batter until completely coated, then drop in deep fryer for 3 – 4 minutes at 350° F, or until golden brown. Drain and serve.

Spicy Mango Salsa

Ingredients:

Mangoes, diced small (3 Each)

Red onion, diced small (1 Each)

Red pepper, diced small (1 Each)

1/6 cup chives, chopped

½ cup cilantro, chopped

1 jalapeno, minced

1 tsp. Cayenne pepper

½ cup apple cider vinegar

Method:

Place chopped ingredients in mixing bowl and mix thoroughly. Then chill before serving.

The mango salsa goes well with the coconut shrimp

Maria's Roman Delight Sandwich

Ingredients:

12" loaf crusty Italian bread, toasted (1 Each)

1" thick slices eggplant (1 Each)

Sliced baked honey ham (2 Each)

Sliced provolone cheese (2 Each)

Breaded, fried chicken tenders (4 Each)

2 large eggs

½ cup milk

4 oz. breadcrumbs (Italian)

3 tbsp. marinara sauce

Method:

Slice bread and toast on grill/flat top. Set aside. Take eggplant, dip it in flour, then egg wash, then Italian breadcrumbs. Sauté for 2 - 3 minutes on each side (until golden brown). Assemble sandwich, beginning with ham, cheese, then eggplant, topped with tenders. On top pieces of bread, spread marinara sauce.

This recipe was developed & used at my apartment complex. Every once in a while I'd make lunch for the management and staff of the apartment complex, I lived in.

CHAPTER 10

Out On My Own

After three successful years at the Holiday Inn in Banner Elk, North Carolina, I decided to begin my own company. I wanted to stay in the hospitality business, so I began a hospitality management company called, "Overlook Hospitality Management, LLC." I picked up two accounts shortly after starting the company. The first was going to be an upscale casual restaurant in a historic facility in Banner Elk. This was a neat idea for a couple reasons. First, Banner Elk was the center of a circle of private wealthy country clubs. Famous athletes and business executives had summer and winter homes at the clubs. Dignitaries from the world of golf, NASCAR and the NFL had homes in the area. Secondly, there were plenty of four diamond restaurants in the area, but no casual restaurants with a variety of high-quality menu items that were nowhere as costly as the four diamond facilities. In addition, this new restaurant would convert into a nightclub on Fridays and Saturdays, complete with an incredible sound system and lighting only seen in the large metro areas like New York City and Miami. There was a baby grand piano in the dining room. During dining hours, a piano player would play show tunes and light jazz. Since we were in the mountains, we used butcher paper on the dining room tables. The paper was changed after each use. At 10 PM, all the tables were stripped completely and used as cocktail tables. We partitioned off a small section for a private parties. They would have their own server and would purchase their liquor by the bottle, sometimes by the Magnum.

The walls of the restaurant were 3D. When the color lights float across the room, it made the light show even more spectacular. The main bar's top was over 40 feet long and was made of 6-inch solid concrete. The contractor spent 2 days sanding the top of the bar, which gave it the look of marble. About every 4 feet of concrete, LED lights were placed. It was designed to produce the colors of the rainbow. When the bartender made cocktails, they would place the cocktails on top of the LED lights, giving off a variety of colors to your drink. Of course, we had several 60-inch flat screen TVs located strategically in areas of the room. They were hooked up to the sound system to add the entertainment factor.

The 2nd property was an upscale Italian restaurant. It was located in the center of town, only yards from the only signal light in town. The kitchen was open for people to see their pizzas being tossed. The first item on my To Do List was to come up with black board chef features that were low carb. More than 50% of the dinner business came from the private clubs in the area. One neat feature of the dining room was the construction of the tables. All were covered with hammered copper. They were gorgeous and required no tablecloth. The background music consisted of songs featuring Frank Sinatra, Tony Bennett, and Perry Como. The wines were fantastic! They included selections from the Antinori wine collection. Chefs from Italy were imported for authenticity. The service was simple, but precise training was an ongoing event, especially wine tastings, and selling the chef's featured selections. A taste of the featured dinners were presented for tasting during the server lineup. The service people were checked for cleanliness of uniforms, fingernails, makeup, and jewelry. It was strict, but that's the difference between good service and great service, plus it was expected by the clientele.

Not too many people know that North Carolina is the 6th largest wine producing state in the country. To that extent, we looked into and bought a blueberry farm vineyard. Blueberries were used on this farm to make a wine called "iced wine." Ice wine is made from fruit left on the vine for one or two frost events. This not only shrunk some of the moisture from the fruit, but it makes the juice from the fruit sweeter. Sweet wines are great for after dinner or dessert wines. Next, we built a winery on the property to produce the "ice wine." We added a retail outlet to sell the wines from the farm. Next, we built a turn-of-the-century Victorian Bed and Breakfast on the site. The Victorian Inn included 8 suites, complete with hot tubs in each suite, flat screen TV's (this was a novel idea in 2002) and fireplaces in each. Approximately $520,000 was spent on furniture for each suite. We opened and suites went for $300 a night. The point-of-sale system was also state of the art, with a web page for the winery. We applied for a helicopter landing pad and permit from the FAA. We had use of a private helicopter to pick up guests from nearby airports from as far away is Charlotte Douglas International Airport. There were English Double Decker buses to take groups of guests to local attractions such as Grandfather Mountain and shopping. Over the coming years, the winery scored several gold medals for their wines.

After a successful venture for the management company, I sold it for a profit and moved back to Florida. The winters in the mountains were brutal, and it was tough to look at leafless trees for more than half the year. I landed a position as a property manager for a timeshare company. The first job I was sent to was in Palm Coast, FL. Palm Coast is located about halfway between Daytona Beach and St-Augustine. There is no business industry located in Palm Coast, and no major companies at all. I'm not sure why someone would come to Palm Coast, but Daytona Beach and Saint Augustine are a 45-minute drive away. Palm Coast is not a cheap place to live. I ran a resort for a timeshare. Timeshares are vacation places where you pay on arrival. The maintenance fee and the condo are free. What no one tells you is that the maintenance fees cost as much as a week at a hotel or a resort. There is a big advantage though. The condo has 1 to 3 bedrooms, a living room, dining room, kitchen and one or two bathrooms. So, it does feel like a vacation home. So, why were timeshare owners always angry? Perhaps it is due to the owners getting hit with what seemed like annually specific assessments sometimes in four figures. The owners were told at the annual meetings of the assessments about upgrades and remodeling, etc. Yet, they never happened. So, where did the money go? I'm not sure, but I did hear about the multi-million-dollar addition to the offices of the timeshare company. The fact that the officers were a family, and each member drove $100,000 sports car, that issue couldn't be dispensed. Since the timeshare owners could never reach the sites, after the purchase my staff and I received the blunt force of their anger. Every Saturday, there were a lot of owners waiting to see me to complain that the limited services were not what they purchased. Saturday became known as refund day. I spent three years with the timeshare company, which was two years too much.

Garlic Pasta
(Serves 1 - 2)

Ingredients:

4 oz. vermicelli pasta (will cook into 8 oz.)

2 Italian plum tomatoes, diced the size of your thumb nail

Imported olives cut in half (6 Each)

½ tsp. of minced garlic (you can buy minced garlic in the produce section at the store)

3 tbsp. extra virgin olive oil

1 tbsp. Lea & Perrins

Salt & pepper to taste

Grated parmesan cheese

1 oz. margarine

Method:

In a fairly large saucepan, fill with water and put on high heat. Add salt to the water and a little margarine. When it comes to a boil, put pasta in and cook al dente, (cooked, but still firm). When cooked, put in colander and rinse with cold water. Place back into saucepan, then add all other ingredients under medium heat. Mix thoroughly and serve.

Another lighter option vs. using a red sauce.

Buffalo Chicken Sandwich
(Serves 2)

Ingredients

6 oz. chicken breasts (2 Each)

2 oz. Italian breadcrumbs

2 oz. Buffalo wing sauce (See recipe on other page)

2 oz. Butter

2 hamburger buns

2 oz. Ranch or Bleu cheese dressing (I prefer Ranch)

Salt and pepper to taste

Method:

Butter rolls and toast on grill or sauté pan. Set aside. Next pound out chicken breasts until flat (to evenly cook), add breadcrumbs and sauté in pan with melted butter until golden on each side (3 - 4 minutes per side). Remove from grill and toss in a bowl with Buffalo wing sauce. Place on bun and drizzle dressing on top.

Spinach & Artichoke Dip
(Serves A Party Of 15 – 20)

Ingredients:

8 oz. cream cheese, room temp

8 oz. heavy cream

4 oz. grated parmesan cheese

4 oz. sour cream

10 oz. frozen chopped spinach, thoroughly drained

4 oz. artichoke hearts

3 oz. chopped red onion

2 tbsp. Franks Hot Sauce

2 tbsp. Lea & Perrins

Fresh cracked pepper to taste

Method:

In a mixing bowl, mix cream cheese, cream, parmesan, spinach, artichoke hearts, red onion, Frank's, Lea & Perrins, and pepper thoroughly. Place into baking dish and put into pre-heated oven at 350°F, for 15 minutes. Remove when hot and serve with chips.

This is a great addition to a party, picnic, etc.

Sicilian Salad
(Serves 2)

Ingredients:

1 medium tomato, or 2 large plum tomatoes

1 medium cucumber

1 green pepper

½ red onion

2 tbsp. feta cheese, chunked

1 tsp. brown or spicy mustard

3 tbsp. balsamic vinegar

1 tbsp. extra virgin olive oil

Salt and pepper to taste

Method:

Dice tomato, cucumber, pepper, and onion the same size and put into salad bowl, Sprinkle cheese over mix. Pour in rest of ingredients and toss lightly until thoroughly mixed. Serve in a bowl with plenty of vinaigrette. Use warm garlic bread to soak up dressing.

I love salads. So, I wanted to make something different to avoid boredom.

Balsamic Salad Dressing
(Makes ½ Cup)

Ingredients:

¼ cup balsamic vinegar

1/8 cup extra virgin olive oil

Salt and pepper to taste

1 tbsp. brown or spicy mustard

Method:

In a mixing bowl, add all ingredients and mix thoroughly. Then pour over salad and toss.

I came up with this recipe to accent my tomato and mozzarella salad.

CHAPTER 11

Back To The Beach

My next stop was to Daytona Beach, where I landed a position as general manager of an oceanfront hotel. In 2004 and 2005, Daytona got hit with four hurricanes. The beachfront was littered with closed hotels, bars, and restaurants. When I arrived in 2007, it still looked like a bomb hit it. I was placed on a hotel in a prime location. Although the hotel hadn't been renovated in many years, it did killer business simply due to its location. The staff were friendly, and the hotel had longtime families visit each year. The hotel companies that owned the hotel owned some 26 hotels on the beach. Their idea was to buy up as many of the beachfront hotels as possible. Once legalized gambling was permitted, they would build as many high-rise hotels as possible. The one flaw in the plan was that the Florida legislator never legalized gambling

The first major event was the Rolex 24-Hour Race, at Daytona Speedway. As it says, it's a 24-hour race held over the weekend a few weeks before the kickoff of the NASCAR season. The Daytona 500 is the first race of the season. I had been on the job for just about a week when the Rolex race occurred. I was living on the property. About 11:30 PM, I was awakened by the phone. It was the night auditor telling me he was quitting. I told him I would be right down to talk to him. Although I had never met this auditor, he accused me of various crimes including no communication, making up new policies and procedures, and the list went on. I responded, "I have never met you what are you talking about?" I managed to calm him down and promised to talk with him first thing in the morning to work out his grievances. I then went back to bed. I had just fallen back to sleep when the phone rang again. It was the auditor giving me 5 minutes to get my butt down to the front desk or he was walking out. This time, he was jumping up and down screaming at me. He said he was leaving, to which I responded, "Don't let the door hit you, where the good Lord split you on the way out." First, I had no idea how this front desk system worked; therefore, I was not able to perform the audit. To make matters worse, we had a new parking lot attendant on duty for the first shift with the hotel. About 12:30 AM, the attendant came into the lobby to tell me he had a headache and was going home. We had 70 parking spots for 101 rooms. We were sold out 100% and it seemed like every guest's room had at least 2 cars. The guests literally plugged up the entire lot including both entrances. I seriously considered walking out myself, but I didn't.

First, I called the assistant general manager. After three calls, she returned my call to let me know she was on the way. When she arrived, she took one look at the parking lot. Her response was "Oh my God!" That was an understatement! Her recommendation was to call Pepo. He was just terminated for cussing at guests. Great! When Pepo arrived, he said he'd have the lot cleared in 30 minutes. Well, it took 45 minutes, but he did it. He called each guest room since there were no parking tags for the cars. He told the guests to move their cars. Some initially refused. Then came the cussing. "Ok," Pepo said, "Get your car or it will be towed, and it will cost you $150 to get your car back." All of a sudden room doors opened, and men came running downstairs in their pajamas and moved their cars. Simply amazing. What was really amazing was the fact that if there was an emergency, no fire truck or emergency vehicle could have made it into our parking lot. Someone could have gone to jail. The next morning, Sunday, the guests checked out very angry. The F bombs between Pepo and the guests went back and forth as they left Daytona. The only other incident from the Rolex weekend was when a guest came to me and asked why his big Ford Dully was in the street? He did park illegally in front of the dumpster with the big no parking signs, and his truck was in the middle of the street. He was most angry due to the fact that it looked like his big 6,000 lb. truck was on the street and the transmission might've been damaged. He was the second person that night to scream and yell at me. That was my first week on the job. Thankfully, it did get better.

The next group to arrive were the bikers for Bike Week with approximately 600,000 bikes. In all actuality, they were a great group. There were bikes of all kinds, some worth six figures. They liked my hotel because we had underground parking for 12 cars. We fit 155 bikes in those 12 parking spots. The only issue we had happened on the last night of bike week was when we turned the clocks forward of course. Everyone got drunk on the last night, and ended up being late checking out, due to daylight savings time. That Sunday was the beginning of Spring Break. At 12 noon, some 150 Spring Breakers were arrived at the hotel lobby with all their baggage.

Since there was a great deal of damage the prior year, we decided to charge a $150 per person damage fee. So, for example if there were 5 people in a room, we'd collect $750 for that room. We had over $20,000 cash in the safe in the form of damage deposits. It was amazing that the damage was very minimal. We had to shampoo the carpets in a few guest rooms where someone had been sick. Other than that, it was a victory! Thank goodness the families arrived after Spring Break ended, and we experienced normality.

About six months into that hotel job, I was promoted to a much larger hotel with 200 plus guestrooms, still on the beach. I walked into a well-maintained hotel with veteran staff. The Chief Engineer and Executive Housekeeper were husband and wife. That usually scared me, but this was different. The couple were from the Czech Republic. They both worked for the same employment company as contract workers. Our hotel was known for the cleanliness on the beach side. The executive housekeeper walked right along with the ladies to ensure they were efficient and thorough. I lived at the hotel as well. I had a two-bedroom suite with two baths, two walk in closets, a full kitchen, and a living and dining room the size of most regular guest rooms. The neatest thing about my suite was the 20-foot balcony across the ocean side, and the 20-foot balcony on the Southside. This was very special because I could watch this space shuttle from my balcony on the 6th floor. Wow! We had a 66,000-gallon pool between the hotel and the beach, one of the largest pools on the whole beach. Since this hotel was located in Daytona Shores, we had a full house during Spring Break. We kept a full house during Bike Week as well. Little did I know, my hotel was the headquarters of the "Outlaws." I met the head biker from the "Outlaws." He was very nice. He informed me that we didn't need security for Bike Week. They supplied the security for the hotel unofficially. It was a quiet week for security. The only incident that happened during the first weekend was when there were 4 to 5 outlaws sitting in the lobby and a couple of civilians checked in at the front desk. One of the two was a bit of a butt head. He demanded a roll away bed. If you don't reserve one, they are rented out on a first come first serve basis. This man starts yelling at my front desk clerk to the point that she began to cry. Watching this, the outlaws got up from their seats and surrounded the angry man. They asked the man if he had a problem? Perhaps he would like the "Outlaw" men to tuck him into his bed. Just those kind friendly words from the outlaw guests made this civilian back away with no more words. The next morning, he came up to me and apologized for the lady at the front desk.

We had a two-level parking facility at the hotel. All of the general managers were asked to find ways to make incidental income during Bike Week. Considering that Daytona has several gentlemen's clubs, I went to the largest of the clubs at the time. I asked a couple of the dancers if they would like to make some extra money for Bike Week doing a bikini wash. They liked the idea and brought some of their friends. We set up a portable bar with keg beer, a grill for barbecue ribs that was smoking up a storm. Then we put out hoses, buckets, and rags. The ladies came in their bikinis, and we took pictures of the girls on the bikes and sold the photos for $10. The dancers made a bunch of money and even more in the evening. This was due to the fact that they had made friends with the bikers that day. We averaged $3,000 a day during bike week, more than any other hotel in the company. About halfway through bike week, my boss the vice president of operations called me and asked me what I was doing to create such income? When I told him, he flipped out. In his words, this is a family hotel to which I replied there are no families this week. There was silence on the phone. He didn't condone what I did but he was impressed with the income. Just about that time I responded it's better to ask for forgiveness than ask for permission.

Within the 5 years at that hotel, I managed to save over $25,000 just by not paying rent and utilities. It also gave me money to do nice things for my staff. The first Christmas, I invited the whole team up to my apartment on the 6th floor. I made a German Christmas dinner of Beef Rouladen with burgundy sauce, sautéed red cabbage with red apples and red onions, red wine and brown sugar cinnamon with nutmeg, and Au Gratin potatoes. For dessert, chocolate chip bread pudding with bourbon sauce. I considered the evening a success since no one jumped off the balcony into the pool from the six floor. As a result of the party, I organized for the monthly employee lunch, the company did not have a budget for employee lunches, so I had to pay for it myself. Seeing the corporate people, I invited for lunch attempt to find out where I was taking the money from to provide the monthly lunches was fun. Despite their busy schedules, they easily made time to visit every 2nd Wednesday of the month at noon.

I was visited one day by a man I had previously known during my management of the first hotel for our company. The man ran the beach buggy concession in front of the hotel. We'd have morning coffee and a cigar before the day began. He asked if I could put him up for a night or two while he found a job. He had just returned from New Orleans after the funeral of his daughter. According to him, the owner of the buggy concession would not let my friend take time off. In fact, he was fired when he attended his daughter's funeral in the "Big Easy." I told him I would put him up and I paid for his room. It got to be more than just a day or two, so I told him I needed some kind of payment. He agreed, and then told me that he got a job and would have a paycheck in less than two weeks. He borrowed my car from time to time at the old hotel, so I thought nothing of it when that evening, he asked to borrow my car to get his paycheck to pay me. I gave him my key. The next morning, I'm having my coffee and cigar like always outside, when something told me to check my parking place, so I did. There was no car. I sent my executive housekeeper up to his room. It was cleared out, and he was gone with my car. We called the Daytona Beach Police and reported the missing vehicle. A detective showed up and questioned me like I was the thief, not the victim. Afterward, the detective warned me that if I was lying, I would be charged with a felony. Finally, he left, and I never heard from the police department after that. Months go by. Finally, I heard from Chrysler Financial who carried the lease on my car. They found my car off I-10 just north of New Orleans. My ex-buddy had stolen my car and drove it until it ran out of gas and left it in a grocery parking lot. The key was still in the ignition, and the battery was dead. Apparently, the local police had it towed to an impound lot where it sat for almost 3 months, collecting storage fees. I called my insurance company and they arranged to pick up the car and bring it back to Daytona. Fortunately, he left the car in perfect condition, and just needed a ride home. Three days after I received the car, I traded it in for a new car.

Fresh Berries w/Sour Cream
(Serves 4)

Ingredients:

2 cups fresh raspberries

2 cups fresh blackberries (for color contrast)

1 pt. heavy cream

1 pt. sour cream

1/8 cup sugar or 4 Splenda packets

Method:

In one mixing bowl, dump berries. In a second mixing bowl, add the rest of the ingredients and thoroughly mix. Add cream mixture to berries and chill before serving.

This is a light ending, but fresh, to any meal.

Cuban Sandwich
(Serves 1)

Ingredients:

1 loaf Cuban bread, cut into 10" sections

3 oz. sliced ham

3 oz. sliced Swiss cheese

3 oz. pulled pork (you can use pulled pork recipe from BBQ recipe or use recipe on

other page)

1 oz. brown mustard

Dill pickle slices (enough to top meat in sandwich)

Method:

Assemble sandwich. First, slice bread down the middle. Then, add ham, cheese, pulled pork, and pickles. Spread mustard over top of a piece of bread (use Italian bread if Cuban bread is unavailable). Put top on sandwich and place in sandwich press. If not available, use a flat electric grill with a weight on top of sandwich. Turn over when bottom is browned to brown top of sandwich. Remove sandwich and cut sandwich on a 45°angle. Serve with a side.

When a Cuban sandwich is made right, you can't beat it!

Deli Rueben Sandwich
(1 Sandwich)

Ingredients:

2 slices of pumpernickel bread or rye

6 – 8 oz. thinly sliced corned beef

2 oz. sauerkraut

2 slices Swiss cheese

2 oz. 1,000 Island dressing (recipe on another page)

Method:

Butter the outside of the bread and place on hot griddle. Add corned beef, Swiss cheese, and sauerkraut (in that order) on one slice of bread. On a second slice of bread, spread 1,000 Island Dressing, then place it on top of the other piece of bread, turn over with spatula to brown other side of sandwich. Serve with a side.

If you even go to a great Jewish deli, such as Katz in NYC, this sandwich is second to none.

CHAPTER 12

Back To The Beginning (Sort Of)

In the aftermath of the company's total collapse, a bank foreclosure, I contacted my mentor, Michael Gibson. I asked if he knew of any job openings in Tennessee. By this time, Mr. Gibson's success really began. He started his own hotel company called M. Gibson Hotels, LLC. He owned and managed approximately fourteen hotels. Before Thanksgiving in 2011, I traveled to Knoxville to have a meeting with Robert Webster (Vice President), Mr. Gibson (President), and their managing partner. In March of 2012, I took over as the General Manager of the Holiday Inn Express in Kodak, Tennessee. The hotel was three years old at the beginning of my tenure. Although it was relatively a new hotel, they had received no awards to their credit. My predecessor, who opened the hotel, was not concerned with winning awards. They seemed less concerned with the needs of each department and was more concerned with the size of the bonus.

Upon taking over, I initially held a full team meeting. It was a simple meeting where the employees complained about a lack of tools to do their jobs and the management's lack of interest. We had several opportunities for improvement. To reinforce our foundation, we established routine weekly meetings with the managers, organized monthly luncheons for the hotel staff, and implemented a consistent training program for the department's uniforms. Surprisingly, we even ensured the availability of laundry soap for the laundry department. They ran out of soap mid-month and were told by the previous general manager their wasn't money in the budget to purchase additional soap. We ordered more soap. More importantly, I printed out each department's monthly budget and provided it to each department head. How can you train a manager of budgets if they never seen one? Suddenly, the deep dark secret of the budget was lifted. I spent time with all the managers on how to use their budgets. My managers found they had money for all the tools they needed to do their jobs including purchasing uniforms. I could see my team's attitude changing. The next item on the agenda was to have a team meeting to discuss our goals. First, of course, was how we would win a "Torchbearer Award." After gaining acceptance from the team, we got everyone's commitment to achieve this goal.

We had a fairly strong housekeeping department. Our executive housekeeper, Angela, taught her employees well. We had some issues at our Front Desk, but our food area was the most in need of change. Our guest service scores ranged from the mid 60% to the mid 70% range. This was pretty sad. We began revising the monthly cleaning. It was filled and left in my mailbox daily. More so, I spent every morning in the kitchen and dining areas training after receiving comments from guests. Our scores began to improve, but not fast enough for me. So, I began holding contests to give out bonuses to each department. Holiday Inn set up an elaborate but easy scoring system. It showed the overall guest service score compared to similar hotel brands in the United States. Scores from particular departments were broken down to make it easy to point out each department's progress. We set cash bonuses for each department's progress. First, housekeeping won their monthly goal. Everyone wants a cash bonus, and word got around fast! Then, the Front Desk won their contest and lastly, the Food Department.

Next, we re-implemented the employee luncheon. Again, my predecessor had abandoned the idea of a luncheon. Initially, there was no money in the budget. . .FAKE NEWS! This time, instead of giving them the same old pizza, I made my team lunch. Everything from Asian, Mexican, Italian, and German to regional American, but NO PIZZA! No one called in sick on Employee Luncheon Day! There was only one stipulation during lunch, you had to sit with people from other departments – what a novel idea! At Christmas and Thanksgiving, we had the full holiday menus from soup to nuts. At Christmas, I also reintroduced the adopted family promotions. This had become a labor of love from the years at the Holiday Inn in Banner Elk, North Carolina. Our housekeeping ladies were in charge of clothing for our adopted kids. They already knew the sizes of the children. Our front desk team got the toys and games. The food department arranged the groceries. First, we bought staple items in bulk from our company grocery vendor. Then, we bought enough fresh food for the family's Christmas dinner. Every year we made one family happy. One year, we even made one of our own happy. One of our housekeeping ladies had 3 children and no spare money to make a cheery Christmas. So, we teamed up and made it extra special that year. The housekeeping lady sacrificed not having a winter coat for herself so that her kids could have one. We pretended to be doing our Christmas shopping for another family with 3 boys like her kids, all the same ages and sizes. When we surprised her, she burst into tears! Then of course so did everyone else!

As the first year ended, we waited intently as the guest service scores were published. We qualified for a "Torchbearer Award." All was going well until we got a new Regional Manager. Let's call him Mr. X. I think he was missing an X chromosome. I was set off by the fact that I lived at the hotel and worked 7 days a week to ensure that we won the award. I had a medical procedure to clean up some loose cartilage in my knee. My doctor instructed me to walk as often as possible to rehab my knee. One afternoon, I popped outside to walk the parking lot before it got dark. Since it was late January, it got dark about 4:30 PM in the mountains. Supervisor X called a few minutes before 4:00 PM and the front desk person told him I had left. He wrote a nasty email to me telling me how disappointed he was in me for leaving work so early. He promised me he would sit in my hotel lobby every day until 5PM to ensure it did not leave early. I called X and suggested he removed his head from his backside and do something constructive with his time rather than follow me around. Things did not improve so I gave my notice and left the company. Some three weeks go by, and I received a call from an old buddy, Fred, from the Hilton Garden Inn. The Hilton was going through a reset within the food and beverage program and Fred wanted to know if I'd be interested in helping put the new program into place. Fortunately, this hotel was still within the Gibson Hotel family. I was cooking again! Or so I thought. There was a reason I went from an executive chef's position to management and that was due to standing on concrete floors for 12 to 14 hours per day. Between both knees needing total replacement and my back, I was in serious pain. However, I was on the job every day. The pain got so bad, that I was taking pain medicine and had a knee brace on each knee and a back support belt on the same time. I even went to the chiropractor every day for adjustments.

Thank goodness a General Manager's position opened up at the Marriott Hotel directly across the street from my old Holiday Inn Express. This was another nice hotel, but the guest service scores were suffering from a lack of urgency. Nationally, the hotel was ranked about 408 out of 720 hotels in that brand that used the same methods I did when the Holiday Inn ascended through the ranks. Within six months, we raised our ranking to the 18th spot nationally. During that time, our Assistant General Manager was brought into train, and it worked out that he would take over for me upon my exit. My heart was truly back at the Holiday Inn across the street. At first, my Assistant General Manager didn't want to listen to me. In fact, he had a tendency to question and argue with my decisions. He went to our Regional Manager, a new one this time, to complain, but the regional suggested he listen to me. A couple days went by, and my assistant came to me. He told me that he disagreed with my decision from the beginning, but our Regional Manager told him to listen to me and to do as I said. My assistant told me he was wrong to question my decisions. He also said that every decision I made turned out to be correct. I thought it was very positive that he confessed he had been wrong. We became close after that. Two months later, he became the new General Manager at the Marriott. I was back at the Holiday Inn, this time without Mr. X looking over my shoulder. Apparently, he had been reassigned back to a General Manager position. It was nice to be back in what I considered it my hotel!

Almost everyone was still at their positions with one exception. My Assistant General Manager at this hotel was transferred to other hotels. She was unhappy and we missed her, so we convinced our corporate people that we should put the management team completely back together and they did.

During my absence, the hotel did lose their 'Torchbearer" status. The General Manager that took my place either didn't know how to maintain a winning team or didn't care. They changed policies and procedures, eliminating all the business contests, saying it was not in the budget. Does that sound familiar? It took over a year to get everyone's head back into the game, but with a lot of patience and retraining we won our second "Torchbearer Award"...my 4th! The great thing about winning awards is not just an ego thing, but it has other benefits. First, it is a huge boost for the morale of my team. It's so nice to have guests come up to the front desk and compliment the team for their quality of service. Secondly, our guests look for award-winning hotels when they plan their trips. They especially look at TripAdvisor for other guest comments. As a result, they are more likely to book their stay at that hotel. Lastly, better service allows the management to charge more, hence increasing their bottom line. It is truly amazing how few General Managers realized this basic premise.

Every year management has the opportunity to recognize chief members for their outstanding contributions. The second year at the Holiday Inn, I nominated my front desk supervisor as the employee of the year through the Tennessee Hospitality Tourism Association. I wrote a narrative about all of my supervisors' accomplishments and how they went above and beyond our guests' expectations. One time, we had an elderly couple staying with us. The wife was quite sickly. My supervisor offered to go to the CVS Pharmacy to pick up her medicines. When she returned to the hotel, she put the medicines on a tray, made her a pot of tea, and toasted an English muffin. Then she brought it to our guest room. The little elderly lady was so thankful and surprised that someone would go that far out of their way to make someone feel better. She wrote a letter to both the ownership and Holiday Inns North America. My supervisor won the best employee award for the region. She also received a cash award from ownership

The second recognition, two years later, went to our executive housekeeper. I nominated her through the same organization for the "Manager of the Year Award." Angela was the hardest working executive housekeeper I had ever worked with in all my years in the business. To her credit, the hotel constantly scored 99% and 100% on both our health inspections as well as our Holiday Inn inspections. Also, to her credit, we took the lst place trophy in the annual Housekeeping Olympics. We competed against 30 other hotels in the region for the title of "Best Housekeeping Department in the County." This was in the resort area of

Gatlinburg, TN. Angela won the manager of the year award for the region. A few weeks later, I received a call from Nashville. It was the Tennessee chapter and the headquarters of the association. They called to say that Angela had also won the "Manager of the Year Award" for the entire state of Tennessee! My team shared their happiness with all our regular guests. The guests in turn congratulated Angela personally. I'd take that any day over dealing with guest complaints!

One day, shortly after all the hoopla, I received a call from one of our national regional reservation centers in Charleston, SC. The gentleman on the line asked me if I could fix him and his family up with a reservation for 4 days. He told me he selected our hotel due to the fact that our hotel received the most calls for booking reservations of any Holiday Inn in the whole region. He wanted to find out just why people wanted to stay at our hotel. I set him up with a reservation. Upon his arrival, he was greeted with a big smile from our front desk team. I was immediately summoned to the desk where I could meet our guests. I gave them a tour of the hotel, plus I spent awhile informing he and his family about the local attractions, including Dollywood and the Great Smoky Mountains National Park. They had a wonderful visit. Upon checking out, I was again summoned to the front desk. The family wanted to personally thank me. The gentleman stressed how friendly and accommodating my team had been to his family. His last comment was the icing on the cake. He said he truly understood why our hotel was asked for the most in the region. His words made my team and I float like a cloud. It was all worth it!

In the fall, tragedy struck in the area. Two underage boys were playing with matches in the mountains. The fire took off in a matter of an hour or two. Hundreds of acres were in flames. The fire spread to Gatlinburg overnight. It burned thousands of businesses and homes. Several people lost their lives. Wind gusts were up to 90 miles per hour through the peaks and valleys. It was so bad that the main road through Gatlinburg was closed off.

Literally 3,000 to 5,000 people were left homeless. I instructed our front desk to cooperate with the authorities with housing the victims. A couple days later, I arrived at the hotel and made my rounds to my department first to ensure all of my team was not affected, and then to inform them that we needed to be aware of the situation. As I walked into the breakfast area, I noticed one lady guest had no shoes on her feet. The toddler in her arms had no shoes as well. Since it was contrary to the Health Department rules to be barefoot where food is served, I diplomatically walked up to our guest and brought it to her attention. She immediately burst into tears. I realized, right at that moment, this was most likely a fire victim. I felt like a big jerk. "Were you in the fire?" I asked. She said she and her family barely escaped death and ran when the fire circled their home. She said they only had time to run with only the clothes on their backs, no shoes. I can't believe I didn't put two and two together. How dumb am I? Minutes later, her husband came down the elevator with their second child. I apologized a dozen times, but it didn't make me feel any better. What can I do to make them more comfortable? The first thing I did was tell the family they had a home at our hotel for as long as they needed...no charge. The next item was to find shoes for them all. I called the local shoe store, gave the store manager my credit card number, and instructed him to fix the family up with warm comfortable shoes. I made sure they got all the breakfast they wanted. After breakfast, I got in touch with the head of the Red Cross who happened to be staying at our hotel. A couple days later, they had temporary housing and more clothes than they could wear. A couple days later, I received a phone call from the mother's father. He called to personally thank my staff for what we did. I told the gentleman that I deserved no thanks and apologized to him for making his daughter cry. I'll never forget that incident.

Stuffed Pork Chop
(Serves 2)

Ingredients:

2 (at least 1" – 1 ½" thick) pork chops, bone in

2 tbsp. Feta cheese, crumbled.

4 oz. spinach timbale mixture (See recipe)

3 oz. butter

Salt & pepper to taste

Method:

Heat skillet, and place pork chops into sear. Season both sides with salt & pepper. Sear for 4 – 5 minutes on each side, then remove to let cool. When cool, cut pockets in chop from back to bone, and stuff with spinach mixture. Place into pre-heated 350°F oven. Bake for 12 – 14 minutes. Remove from oven and top with feta cheese. Put back into oven to melt cheese. Remove from oven and serve.

Spinach Timbale
(Makes 2 Servings)

Ingredients:

10 oz pkg chopped spinach (frozen/thawed and drained) (1 Each)

2 – 3 tbsp. Grated parmesan cheese

1 heaping tbsp. Sour cream

2 tbsp. Lea & Perrins

1 stick butter

¼ cup breadcrumbs

Salt & pepper to taste

Method:

In a saucepan, place thoroughly drained spinach and melt butter. Stir, then add sour cream (**DO NOT BURN SOUR CREAM**). Add remaining ingredients and mix thoroughly. Maybe used as a vegetable side, or to stuff in meat.

Baked Stuffed Peppers
(Serves 4)

Ingredients:

4 large green peppers, tops cut off & seeded

1 lb. ground chuck

4 oz. long grain rice

½ red onion, chopped

2 oz. Lea & Perrins

Salt & pepper to taste

1 tsp. granulated garlic

1 tbsp. dried basil

3 - 4 oz. lemon juice

1 qt. water

Method:

In a skillet, brown ground beef and onion. Set aside. In a saucepan, cook off rice until al dente, rinse colander with cold water. Let drain. In a mixing bowl, add beef/onions, rice, and seasoning, except for lemon juice and water. With a spoon stuff peppers with mixture. Place stuffed peppers in baking dish. Around sides of peppers pour water & lemon juice. Place dish into preheated 350°F oven and bake for 1 hour. Remove from oven and add a tbsp. of lemon water to mixture inside peppers and serve.

This is a traditional recipe. The kicker is the lemon juice you add to the water when baking in oven. It brings it to another level.

CHAPTER 1

On The Road Again

I had given my notice. I had planned to retire at the end of April 2017. 1 gave my notice 24 months prior. This gave ownership plenty of time to hire and train a new General Manager. As luck would have it, ownership found and hired someone. So, in January of 2017, I was asked to go to Evansville, IN to see what I could do to get their Marriott property back on track.

After a briefing with corporate management, we got everyone together for a meeting. The President, Vice President of Operations, and new Assistant Manager (who happened to be my former Assistant GM from the Marriott across the street from my old Holiday Inn). Their guest service scores were horrible. Turnover was huge. Most of all, the attitude of the whole team was as bad as I had ever seen. This needed more than a motivational speech. There had to be a reason for the low morale.

It didn't take a rocket scientist to figure out where my main issues were stinking up the atmosphere. As good as my housekeeping team was in Knoxville, this team was the pits! I asked Angela to come up for a few days to put policies and procedures in place. She was on the 2nd floor on the first day when she called me on the radio. Angela had sent a room attendant down to the laundry to get a set of sheets. The laundry lady chased the room attendant from the laundry back to the 2nd floor. Angela asked her where the sheets were. The room attendant told Angela that the laundry person had kicked her out without the sheets. I went to the laundry to get the other side of the story. The laundry lady told me that the room attendants were taking all the clean linen up to the floors. I told her that it was their responsibility to do that, and any leftovers will be stored in the linen closets. The laundry lady informed me that it had never been that way before and she wasn't going to stay now. Really!? I gave her a direct order in front of the Executive Housekeeper and Angela to follow through with my original instructions. The laundry lady stated she knew Mr. Gibson personally, and if I gave her anymore stupid instructions, she would have Mr. Gibson straighten me out. So, I gave her Gibson's cell number. She didn't call him, and I thought that the matter was resolved. The next morning, we went through the same dog and pony show. So, I closed the matter by letting her go on the spot.

The other issue was with a young man at our front desk who was made supervisor and transferred from sales. This situation came to an end much quicker.

He ignored his schedule, and I terminated him immediately. All of a sudden, all the chaos subsided. The team began working together and began to smile! The two thorns that were removed had caused all the stress and tensions. Scores began to rebound. We began a spring cleaning in all departments. There was so much paperwork and trash in the G's office that you could not see the desk.

Things were improving, so I decided to do a special lunch for the team. I made sizzling fajitas with homemade guacamole, paella, and shrimp. The whole first floor smelled incredible! There happened to be a couple hotel guests, from another hotel, working on their laptops in the public area. One gentleman popped his head into the kitchen and asked what I was making. He stated it smelled great! So, I invited him and his associate to lunch. They came! After lunch, the one gentleman said, "Due to the fact we were invited to lunch, we will stay at your hotel on our next trip." We exceeded his guest's expectations.

Having improved our guest satisfaction scores and the morale, my next task was to find a replacement G.M. to replace myself. Hopefully, we could find someone within the current staffing plan. Plan B was to find someone from the outside. We were fortunate to have the Guest Service Manager step up to the plate. We discussed what would be expected from ownership and she was ok. So, we entered into some expedited training. She took over when I left.

One month later, I was asked to go to our next troubled spot. It was a Holiday Inn Express outside of Knoxville, TN. The ownership had just removed the G.M. that I was replacing. The first challenge was to deal with the Assistant GM who was the daughter of the G.M who had just been removed. Fortunately, I knew both the old G.M. and the assistant. I always believed that it was better to go into a job without the intention of firing them. So, I worked with her. A few days into my tenure, I noticed my assistant was doing all the ordering from her desk. In addition to that issue, was the fact that we were running out of some supplies and had way too much of the others. For example, we had a years' supply of juice and coffee. I called the vendor, and they took back the items that were not past the sell date, but we were stuck with the produce past the sell date. I was able to sell off more of my overload to other hotels in the company, and stopped ordering those items until we were down to our par level. Office supplies were another mess. We had such a backlog of supplies and there was literally no place to put the inventory. Of course, as soon as I realized my assistant's ordering tactics, I told her not to order anything without my prior knowledge or approval. However, she continued to order in the same manner she was accustomed. That fact alone really ticked me off. I sat down with her to discuss these issues. The discussion seemed to have only one party involved…me.

Next step was to have our Director of Operations get involved. United, we decided to part ways with the assistant. It also became apparent that there were no hiring procedures. The chief engineer was a former utility person with no engineering experience whatsoever. He had no clue how to perform his duties as chief. It was sad to see the condition of the hotel's preventive maintenance program. He was the next to go. He should have never been promoted. The Executive Housekeeper was a good person, just not trained. She had never taken a linen inventory or ordered her own supplies. I brought my old Executive Housekeeper, Angela, for a few days from my award-winning hotel. Angela helped the exec get her act together. Then, I found a new chief engineer. Oh, by the way, the assistant we had terminated was also the Front Desk Manager. Luckily, we had someone on staff that was smart enough to begin training as a supervisor. They were to eventually become the manager of the guest service experience. Two months into the project, we were just turning the corner on "righting this ship." The Evansville project began to turn around in one week by comparison.

The good news, if there was any, as a matter of fact there was. A buddy of mine was going to take over as GM, and my retirement, which was quickly approaching – was less than a month away. I met Taylor during the trip to Manchester, TN. I was to watch the hotel while the current GM took a few days off. It was a very well-kept order Holiday Inn Express. The staff were friendly and helpful, and the place was clean. Just good steady business by the Interstate. Taylor and I worked a couple more times together in Knoxville. The company had just taken over a couple of bank repossessions. One of which, later, turned into a real mess.

It was a case of mismanagement and theft from prior ownership. On the day we took over, Taylor and I walked the property. The first guest room we walked into; Taylor went first – he fell through the floor…literally!

Prior ownership had stretched the carpet over a hole in the floor! The next room, as we walked in, we noticed rays of sunlight. We thought it odd with the curtains being closed. So, we looked up to find a hole in the roof and ceiling. This was getting scary. We went outside to get a breath of fresh air. During our walk, we notice a metal light pole in the parking lot. The cover over the electrical unit was missing. I looked into the pole to find bare wires touching the pole. Imagine a child touching this pole! Instant electrocution! I ordered the power to the poles be shut off, then called the ownership to inform them what I had found. They called some electricians to repair.

It was time for lunch, but actually, neither of us felt like eating. Both our stomachs felt kind of queasy. That afternoon, one of the coworkers of my company found mold in all the rooms facing the water park. What a first day! As the days passed, it just got worse, but that was just my second experience with Taylor. This was just my way of saying I trusted Taylor and his ability to run a hotel.

That brings me to my retirement day – April 30th, 2017. After working at more than half a dozen hotels in my 5 years with Gibson Hotel Management, it was time to get in some fishing and golf. Just before I moved back to Florida, Mr. Gibson and company held a retirement party that far exceeded my expectations! It brought a tear to my eye. In the course of my career, I worked with Michael Gibson five separate times. Michael was there for me through my divorce, and when hotel companies that I worked for went out of business. My career was adventurous, fun, challenging, and filled with hard fought wisdom. I grew as a manager, chef, and as a person with each job. I appreciated them all.

Cherry & Chocolate Chip Bread Pudding w/ Bourbon Sauce

Ingredients for Pudding:

1 cherry coffee cake from bakery, diced and put into baking dish (4" x 4" x 8")

1 pt. heavy cream

¼ cup chocolate chips

2 eggs

1 tbsp. cinnamon

1 tsp. nutmeg

1 tsp. pure vanilla

¼ cup brown sugar

Ingredients for Bourbon Sauce:

½ cup powdered sugar

1 tbsp. Bourbon or rum

1 tbsp. pure vanilla

Method:

In a baking dish, put diced coffee cake. In a mixing bowl, mix all wet and dry ingredients then pour over cake. Make sure to soak all pieces, then place into a preheated 350° F oven. Bake for–35 - 45 minutes, or until done. Put a toothpick into pudding and remove. If it comes out clean, it's done. In another mixing bowl, add all sauce ingredients. Sauce should be thick – it will melt over warm pudding. Serve with Cherry Garcia ice cream (Ben & Jerry's).

No calories, no fat...no carbs...not.
But every once in a while, you have to splurge.

Pineapple Upside Down Cake

Ingredients:

1 box yellow lemon cake mix

1 small can pineapple slices

1 small bottle maraschino cherries (stem removed)

5 oz. brown sugar

5 oz. butter

Whole eggs (3 Each)

½ cup water

1/3 cup canola oil

Method:

Preheat oven to 350°F. Next, melt butter, then add brown sugar to make syrup. When sugar and butter are melted and mixed, pour into bottom of 8" x 9" baking dish. Place pineapple rings in a decorative manner, then place cherries into center holes of pineapple rings. In a large mixing bowl, add contents of cake mix, eggs, water, and oil, Mix thoroughly (no lumps). Add batter to baking dish and spread evenly. Bang baking dish a few times to remove any air bubbles, then place in preheated oven, Bake for–35 - 45 minutes or until golden brown on top. Stick toothpick in center. If it comes out clean, cake is done. Let cake sit and cool for 3 – 5 minutes. Then put platter upside down on top of baking dish, and turnover. Cake should come out right side up, onto platter. Let fully cool and serve.

This recipe was used extensively at the Holiday Inn Express, Kodak, TN for my team. I made a complete lunch for my team every month at their employee lunch.

Spinach & Artichoke Stuffed Poblano Peppers Wrapped w/ Bacon
(Serves 4)

Ingredients:

4 poblano peppers, sliced in half lengthwise

10 oz. package frozen chopped spinach, drained

Marinated artichoke hearts chopped into pieces (4 Each)

½ cup mayo

1/6 cup whipped cream cheese (room temp)

¼ cup sour cream

½ cup grated Parmesan cheese

2 tbsp. Lea & Perrins

Cracked black pepper to taste

8 slices Hickory Bacon

16 plain toothpicks

Method:

Slice peppers lengthwise, and remove seeds (poblanos are mild, similar to green peppers). In a mixing bowl, add rest of ingredients except for bacon. Take mixture and stuff into peppers. Then wrap bacon around stuffed peppers, and secure with toothpicks. Place into baking dish. Put into a preheated oven 350°F. Bake for 1 hour, or until bacon is crisp. Take out of oven and let cool for 10 minutes. Serve.

If you like jalapeno poppers, the poblanos will make it a meal!

Authentic Ham & Bean Soup
(Makes 1 Gallon)

Ingredients:

Bones from bone-in Virginia ham

1 lb. white (navy) beans

3 Medium carrots, diced pieces

½ Spanish onions, diced pieces

3 stalks celery, diced pieces

Salt & pepper to taste

3 lb. ham from leftover Virginia ham, diced

3 qt. water

Method:

Begin by soaking beans overnight in water. The next day, add ham bone with meat on bone. Bring it to a boil and let it cook down until meat falls off bone, and beans are tender. Then add carrots, onion, celery. Soup will thicken up when beans cook down. There is so much flavor from ham bone, you should not have to add season other than a little salt and pepper. If still not proper flavor, add some chicken stock.

*Note: when cooking beans, you may have to add water as beans get tender.

This is one of the best soups I have ever made! it is very important that you use the whole bone with meat on it when cooking it down. All the flavor that comes to the soup is from the bone.

Raspberry/Chocolate Chip Bread Pudding

Ingredients:

Raspberry, (or any other flavor), coffee cake (1 Each)

1 bag chocolate chips

1 pt. heavy cream

1 tbsp. ground cinnamon

1 tbsp. ground nutmeg

1 tbsp. real vanilla

4 oz. brown sugar

Large eggs (3 Each)

Rum Sauce:

1 ¾ oz. powdered sugar

½ oz. dark rum

Mix together and pour over pudding after cooled

Method:

Dice raspberry cake into cubes and place into baking dish. Sprinkle ¼ bag of Chocolate Chips throughout. In a mixing bowl place, all other ingredients and mix thoroughly. Pour into baking dish and push any cake under liquid level. Place into preheated 350°F oven and bake for 45 min. or until center is cooked. Let cool, then add glaze sauce over top.

Printed in the USA
CPSIA information can be obtained
at www.ICGtesting.com
LVHW081651200923
758648LV00006B/100

9 781737 691891